BRET HARTE'S CALIFORNIA

Bret Harte circa 1870. (Courtesy of California State Library)

BRET HARTE'S CALIFORNIA

LETTERS TO THE *Springfield Republican* AND

Christian Register, 1866–67

EDITED AND WITH AN INTRODUCTION BY

Gary Scharnhorst

UNIVERSITY OF NEW MEXICO PRESS

Albuquerque

This book is dedicated to George Arms,
a scholar, gentleman, and friend.

Library of Congress Cataloging-in-Publication Data

Harte, Bret, 1836–1902.
Bret Harte's California : letters to the Springfield Republican and
Christian register, 1866–67 / edited and with an introduction by
Gary Scharnhorst. — 1st ed.
p.   cm.
Includes bibliographical references and index.
ISBN 0–8263–1222–5 (cloth)
1. California—History—1850–1950.   2. California—Description
and travel—1848–1869.   I. Scharnhorst, Gary.   II. Springfield
Republican (Springfield, Mass. : 1855 : Daily)   III. Springfield
weekly Republican (Springfield, Mass. : 1854)   IV. Christian register
(Boston, Mass. : 1843)   V. Title.
F864.H318   1990
979.4′04—dc20   90-37423

Design by Kristina Kachele.

Contents

INTRODUCTION   *1*

BIBLIOGRAPHICAL NOTE   *9*

ILLUSTRATIONS   *13*

Letter 1: January 18, 1866, to the *Register*   *19*

Letter 2: January 18, 1866, to the *Register*   *21*

Letter 3: March 9, 1866, to the *Register*   *23*

Letter 4: March, 1866, to the *Register*   *26*

Letter 5: April 5, 1866, to the *Republican*   *28*

Letter 6: April 10, 1866, to the *Register*   *32*

Letter 7: April 20, 1866, to the *Republican*   *35*

Letter 8: May —, 1866, to the *Register*   *39*

Letter 9: June, 1866, to the *Register*   *41*

Letter 10: June 11, 1866, to the *Republican*   *43*

Letter 11: June 30, 1866, to the *Register*   *47*

Letter 12: July 9, 1866, to the *Republican*   *51*

Letter 13: July 14, 1866, to the *Register*   *55*

Letter 14: July 28, 1866, to the *Register*   *58*

Letter 15: August 5, 1866, to the *Republican*   *62*

Letter 16: August 8, 1866, to the *Republican*   *66*

Letter 17: August 18, 1866, to the *Register*   *70*

Letter 18: August 30, 1866, to the *Register*   *73*

Letter 19: August 31, 1866, to the *Republican*   *77*

CONTENTS

Letter 20: September 9, 1866, to the *Republican*   *82*

Letter 21: September 11, 1866, to the *Register*   *86*

Letter 22: September 18, 1866, to the *Republican*   *90*

Letter 23: September 28, 1866, to the *Register*   *94*

Letter 24: September 29, 1866, to the *Republican*   *97*

Letter 25: October 9, 1866, to the *Republican*   *101*

Letter 26: October 9, 1866, to the *Register*   *105*

Letter 27: October 30, 1866, to the *Register*   *108*

Letter 28: February 28, 1867, to the *Republican*   *112*

Letter 29: April 10, 1867, to the *Republican*   *115*

Letter 30: April 15, 1867, to the *Register*   *119*

Letter 31: May, 1867, to the *Republican*   *123*

Letter 32: June 15, 1867, to the *Republican*   *127*

Letter 33: July 29, 1867, to the *Republican*   *130*

Letter 34: August 9, 1867, to the *Republican*   *135*

Letter 35: September 17, 1867, to the *Republican*   *139*

Letter 36: October 8, 1867, to the *Republican*   *144*

Letter 37: November 12, 1867, to the *Register*   *148*

NOTES   *153*

INDEX   *165*

INTRODUCTION

Gary Scharnhorst

FIVE YEARS BEFORE HE BECAME THE HIGHEST paid author in America, Bret Harte grubbed in the literary outback as the California correspondent to two Massachusetts papers. Whereas he would earn a cool ten thousand dollars for writing a baker's dozen poems and stories for the publishing firm of Fields, Osgood & Co. in 1871–72, he received no more than ten dollars for any of the pieces he sent the Boston *Christian Register* and *Springfield Republican* in 1866–67. These thirty-seven essays, varying in length from a few hundred to several thousand words, are like cartloads of raw ore ready to be milled. They are obviously not finished coin, though they display an abundance of "color." In several cases, especially in some of his early articles for the *Register*, Harte seems to be merely prospecting. At their best, however, his letters from California contain nuggets of topical comment and local history quarried from the mother lode, including one of the first notices of Mark Twain in a national publication. Harte gleaned many of these items from newspapers, particularly the San Francisco *Alta California*, the *Morning Call*, the *Evening Bulletin*, the *Sacramento Union*, even the *Montana Post*. Sometimes, as in his account of the hilarious *faux pas* committed by a troupe of Japanese jugglers, his anecdotes seem to be based on first-hand observation if only because they are more complete than newspaper reports of these same events. Occasionally, Harte editorializes on such topics as municipal corruption and the decline of the Union party, the acting style of Edwin Forrest, the visit of Queen Emma of Hawaii, and the sudden collapse of buildings in downtown San Francisco.

A native of New York state, an immigrant to California in 1854 at the age of eighteen, Harte had already won something of a local reputation as a contributor to such San Francisco literary weeklies as the *Golden Era* and the *Californian*. By the happiest of circumstances, he had been taken under wing early in his literary apprenticeship by Thomas Starr King, minister of the First Unitarian Church of San

Francisco. King had left his native New England in 1860 to establish a Unitarian beachhead on the West Coast, and he would prove his fealty to the Union during the Civil War by raising over a million dollars for the U. S. Sanitary Commission. In January 1862, King sent the manuscript of Harte's story "The Legend of Monte del Diablo" to his Boston friend James T. Fields, editor of the *Atlantic Monthly*, with a cover letter recommending its publication:

> Mr. F. B. Harte, a very bright young man who has been in literary ways for a few years, has written a piece, wh[ich] I have not yet seen, but feel sure it is good. . . . I shall read the piece before this note goes. I hope the editors will accept it if it is worthy, for I am sure there is a great deal in Harte, & an acceptance of his piece would inspirit him, & help literature on this coast where we raise bigger trees & squashes than literati & brains.[1]

The story subsequently appeared in the *Atlantic*—the only specimen of his prose Harte would publish outside California before becoming a regular correspondent to the *Register* and the *Republican*—and King would predict in the fall of 1862 in a letter to the *Boston Transcript* that his young parishioner would "yet be known more widely in our literature."[2]

On his part, and by his own testimony, Harte sometimes overlooked Starr King's "heroic proportions" in the "familiar contemplation of his exquisite details."[3] After the minister died suddenly in March 1864, however, Harte paid eloquent tribute to him in three poems—"Relieving Guard," "On a Pen of Thomas Starr King," and "At the Sepulchre," the latter a meditation at King's "modest little tomb" (as he described it in letter 3) beside the church on Geary street.

> And greener yet that spot shall grow,
>   For thy dear dust within it laid,
> And brighter yet the sunlight glow—
>   And dim and grateful seem the shade.[4]

Harte would subsequently name his second son after King and dedicate his first book to King's memory. He would also mention him fondly and frequently in his articles for the *Register* and *Republican*.

Though he had lived in California for a dozen years, Harte assumed the pose in these letters of an expatriate or foreign correspondent.

"When you meet" at "the Eastern borders of the continent," he adjures his readers in letter 18, think "tenderly" of the "unrelieved sentinels at the Western gate." Like a missionary in the field, he attempts to describe the quaint habits and exotic customs normal to "California civilization." The people of the state are gamblers by nature, he reports, famous for fast living and prodigal giving. Like the Arabian Prince, they "prefer their cream tarts with pepper." He has but rarely seen in the unruly West the sort of "neat farm-houses" and manicured farms he remembers in the East. "We have *ranchos* instead of farms" and "*vaqueros* for milk-maids." Harte repeatedly insists that "Californians are naturally cosmopolitan and liberal," "innately liberal," and "wonderfully adaptive," but he ruefully admits that Frederick Law Olmstead's plan for a public common in San Francisco along the lines of Central Park in New York was "too liberal, too large, too comprehensive for this material—and, in such matters, narrow-minded— municipality." He criticizes feminism in the person of a Bloomer—admittedly, the "product of an older civilization and progressive ideas" transplanted from the East—on the grounds that California society "is too material in tone already; we cannot afford to accept any innovation which tends to lower the standard of female modesty." Harte also indicts the subtle restraints on "intellectual life and activity" in the West, even asserting in letter 31 that "the climate is fatal to abstract speculation." California literature will never come of age, he subsequently laments, so long as there are "more writers than readers" and "more contributors than subscribers" in the state.

Harte was also a social liberal who roundly protested racial intolerance and persecution, his apparent ethnocentrism notwithstanding. As a young editor in Humboldt County in 1860, he had quite literally fled for his life after condemning in print a wanton massacre of Indians by white vigilantes near Eureka.[5] By the time he writes these letters, he has become a radical or "black Republican." Despite his tendency to echo racial clichés—e.g., the Chinese are generally "simple and industrious," inscrutable in expression, and pagan in religion— Harte was genuinely sympathetic to the plight of the local Chinese and African-Americans. (He refers only in passing to "our friends, the liberal Mexicans of San Francisco," and he treats "Digger Indians," Polynesians, and Japanese with marked condescension.) Harte adds "patient under abuse" to his list of stereotypical Chinese traits and laments that the "celestials" must "continually" exercise this trait in California. He deplores the "late riots and outrages on the Chinese" in letter 28 and attributes it, not without cause, to class rivalries: the Chinese were gradually supplanting the Irish as menial laborers. He would later recreate these riots in the story "Wan Lee, the Pagan" and satirize ethnic jealousy of the Chinese in the poem "Plain Language from Truthful James." Harte denounces other forms of racial bigotry as well: When blacks are prevented from marching in a parade in order to "spare the sensitive prejudices of our Irish and southern fellow-citizens," he writes, the excluded people bear their "humiliation with dignity and silence." Lest such remarks appear to betray an anti-Irish bias, compare Harte's comments on Fourth of July celebrations in the city in letters 12 and 13. In the more political essay for the *Republican*, Harte explicitly censures Irish societies or clubs such as the Fenians. In the essay to the *Register*, he ignores the Irish entirely. That is, Harte's adversion to things Irish was rooted in differences fundamentally political, not religious or racial.

His ambivalence to things Western extends even to his treatment in these letters of the fabled California landscape. Scarcely a letter appeared in either paper without Harte commenting on the geography or climate of the state, as if these were the subjects he believed Easterners would find most fascinating. He refers to the weather as early as the second sentence of the first letter and, in fact, the passage of the seasons is a sort of subtext that gives these essays an overall continuity. For the most part, Harte subverts the mythology of a paradisiacal California. He confesses in letter 4 that he had "tried for twelve years to appreciate this remarkable climate," albeit to no avail. And in letter 22 he writes grimly of "a country where there is so much clear weather and so few pleasant days." To be sure, Harte depicts Berkeley as a bucolic Eden, a veritable Utopia "where the wind doesn't blow and the fogs come not," a "Xanadu of the San Francisco poetical dream." Elsewhere, however, he warns darkly that the coast is but an "imaginary Utopia" after all—"a country which, more than any other, exacts the greatest labor, endurance, energy and pluck, as the conditions of success."

Harte's columns in the *Register* and *Republican* comprise at least the stuff of stories and poems, if not of dreams. In them, like a wildcat miner, the young writer sampled the soil before staking out a claim. His assay/essay on Mission Dolores in letter 6, for example, is remarkably similar to his "Bohemian Paper" on the same subject in *The Luck of Roaring Camp and Other Sketches*. Stephen Venard, the stagedriver Harte mentions in letter 10, prefigures Yuba Bill, the expressman who frequents his fiction, and his critique of the popular evangelist A. B. Earle in letter 27 anticipates his satire of revivalism in such stories as "Mr. MacGlowrie's Widow." He lampooned the discovery of a prehistoric skull in Calaveras county in letter 15 no less than in his celebrated comic poem "To the Pliocene Skull." His sketch of a California resort community in letter 22 foreshadows the setting of his story "The Reformation of James Reddy." In letter 28, he refers in passing to "Poker Flat," his first allusion to the fictional mining town he would depict in "The Outcasts of Poker Flat" and other stories. Harte later fictionalized in "Maruja" the legal controversy over Spanish land grants he chronicles in letter 24 and in "Colonel Starbottle for the Plaintiff" the breach of promise suit he describes in letter 29. Quite apart from their topical interest, in short, these essays detail the sources of some of Harte's most popular works.

To be sure, he wrote them in part because he needed the money, however modest the amount. In August 1862, he had married Anna Griswold, a contralto in the choir at Starr King's church, and in the spring of 1863, with King's help, he went to work in the U. S. Mint at San Francisco, a *sinecure* he would hold until August 1869 at a salary of upwards of $270 per month.[6] Robert B. Swain, the Superintendent of the Mint, also chaired the Board of Trustees at King's church— Harte would mention "this quiet, blue-eyed man" in his very first letter to the *Register*, the weekly journal of the Boston Unitarians. Swain later acknowledged that he had given Harte the clerkship so that the budding writer might be at liberty to pursue a literary career.[7]

But as Harte's opportunities increased, so too did his obligations: by 1865 he had become the father of two children, and wartime inflation had eroded his clerical salary. In the winter of 1865–66, moreover, he quarreled with C. H. Webb, the owner of the *Californian*, the paper he had intermittently edited and to which he had regularly contributed since its founding in the spring of 1864. Webb seems to have provoked the dispute by panning *Outcroppings*, Harte's edition of California verse, at least three times—in his West Coast correspondence with the *New York Times*, under the pseudonym "John Paul" in the *Sacramento Union*, and under the pseudonym "Inigo" in the pages of the very magazine they had launched together.[8] Harte never forgave the offense. He curtly reported to Webb in October 1866—in the only letter they exchanged still extant—that he had successfully brokered the sale of the *Californian*, and his final lines ooze with sarcasm: "I, in regard to the paper, its present proprietors, & the judiciousness of your bargain say nothing, simply subscribing myself with high regard and considerable satisfaction no longer/Your attorney in fact,/Fr[ank] Bret Harte."[9] Fortunately, Warren Sawyer, the managing editor of the *Christian Register*, had invited him in December 1865 to become a regular contributor to his paper, and Harte had readily accepted on the condition that he receive the same payment he had customarily earned for his articles in California magazines: "I could not write regularly for a less sum than $10 in gold." Though the *Register* usually paid its correspondents only five dollars per essay, Sawyer acceded to Harte's terms. No less a luminary than Mark Twain wrote his mother and sister on January 20, 1866, that Harte had "quit the 'Californian'" to "write for a Boston paper hereafter."[10] A year later, however, Harte complained to Sawyer that he had received only sixty dollars for the twelve letters he had contributed to the paper between May and December 1866: "I think you will agree with me that I had some reason in expecting double the amount."[11] Whether or not this misunderstanding was corrected, Harte wrote only two more pieces for the *Register*, and these last of his contributions to its pages appeared at intervals of several months.[12]

Harte had a less checkered career as a columnist for the *Springfield Republican*. Its owner and editor Samuel Bowles—best known today as a friend of the Dickinson family in nearby Amherst—had traveled overland to California in 1865 in company with Schuyler Colfax, the Speaker of the House of Representatives and a future Vice-President of the United States; William Bross, the Lieutenant Governor of Illinois; and A. D. Richardson of the *New York Tribune*. No less a booster of the New West than Horace Greeley, Bowles wrote a series of sketches about the trip for the *Republican*, later collecting these essays into the type of genteel travelogue Mark Twain satirized mercilessly in *Roughing It*. While in the Bay area, Bowles also tried to recruit a local correspondent to his paper. He initially persuaded Horatio Stebbins, King's successor at the Unitarian Church, to write for him, though Stebbins opined in the one piece he actually published that Bowles had practically exhausted the available topics in his earlier letters from the coast.[13] Under the circumstances, Bowles soon replaced Stebbins with

Harte, whom he no doubt remembered from his western tour the year before—after all, Bowles had visited both the mint where Harte worked and the church he attended.[14]

Whatever his impression of Bowles in the summer of 1865, Harte had curried the editor's favor by plugging his book of western sketches. According to his biographer, Harte free-lanced for several San Francisco newspapers in 1866 and 1867, including the *Alta California*, the *Call*, and the *Bulletin*, though the pieces he wrote for these papers were mostly unsigned.[15] Thus authorship of an anonymous review of Bowles's *Across the Continent* in the *Bulletin* cannot with certainty be attributed to Harte. Still, the notice betrays all the earmarks of Harte's critical style: The book is "one of the most entertaining as well as substantially instructive volumes we have read in many a day," the critic averred, and it "will do much toward enlightening the people of the East as to the capacities, the wants and the future destiny of the Pacific shores."[16] Some circumstantial evidence also points to Harte as the author of the review. He claimed later that he had "praised and defended" *Across the Continent* upon its publication.[17] In any event, this much is certain: Bowles reprinted the "very generous and flattering" notice in the *Springfield Republican* for March 7, 1866; and Harte's first letter to Bowles's paper was dated less than a month later—barely enough time in 1866, before the completion of the transcontinental railroad, for mail from Massachusetts to reach California.

By virtue of the publicity it gave him over the months, the *Republican*, more than any other publication, should be credited with bringing Harte to the attention of Eastern readers. As a featured contributor to its pages, he enjoyed a certain celebrity: As early as September 1866, for example, Bowles reprinted in the paper a "quaint" poem by "our special San Francisco correspondent, Mr. F. Bret Harte,"[18] and in January 1867 he favorably compared Harte to two of his star-crossed western rivals, Webb and Mark Twain: Harte, Bowles insisted,

> is less demonstrative in his qualities than the others; his humor is more subjective, and his scholarship more thorough and conservative; but we have few newspaper and magazine writers in the East that have so charming and cultivated a fancy, so delicate and innocent a satire. He still remains in San Francisco; and is known to our readers through various correspondence during the last year. . . .[19]

Bowles reiterated the point in May 1867: Harte is the "best of the California humorists after all."[20] Webb asked in his own column in the paper (again pseudononymously) why the editors had paid Harte so "equivocal" a compliment "in saying that, *after all*, he is 'the best,'" etc.[21] Two months later, in his only surviving letter to Bowles, Harte bewailed "Webb's refreshing notice of me in his correspondence with the *Republican*" and asked, if only rhetorically, what had "possessed that clever, audacious wretch to roast me" in print for the failure of *Outcroppings*.[22]

Whereas Harte's early letters to the *Republican* mainly boost the West, his late letters betray an increasing dissatisfaction with the region. "The near fact is that we live in a country unpleasantly new and uncomfortably inchoate," he gripes in letter 36. He concludes this letter by promising to discuss in his next essay the "shameful" closure of the college of California and the related "moral and intellectual degeneracy of this country." Such a topic was scarcely what Bowles had in mind when he recruited a San Francisco correspondent, and this last of Harte's letters to the paper was the only one *not* to be reprinted in the weekly edition of the *Republican*. Whether or not Harte wrote the sequel he planned, it was not published in the paper, and the work of a new California columnist would begin to appear in the *Republican* six weeks later.[23]

However, even after Harte wrote the last of his letters to the paper—an affiliation that ended only a few months before he became the first editor of the *Overland Monthly*—he enjoyed a virtual immunity from criticism in its pages. By an odd coincidence, the *Republican* was one of the first Eastern journals to extol the merits of Harte's tale "The Luck of Roaring Camp," published without signature in the *Overland* for August 1868. "The hand that wrote it," according to the paper, "ought to be able to make a book, or at any rate, to 'contribute to every number'" of the new magazine.[24] Three days later, on September 12, 1868, the editors reprinted the tale in its entirety, and by the end of the month they had announced that none other than "our old friend Harte" had written "the best magazine story of the year."[25] Over the next three years, in fact, the *Republican* would welcome each successive issue of the *Overland*;[26] reprint Harte's best work from it, including "The Outcasts of Poker Flat," "Miggles," "Tennessee's Partner," "Mr. Thompson's Prodigal," and "Plain Language from Truthful James";[27] and favorably review his collections of stories and poems.[28] To be sure,

Harte might yet prove to be a flash in the pan, or so the *Republican* sometimes fretted: "It is still an open question whether he will hold out as he has begun."[29] Harte answered with a sort of fusillade in the last *Overland* issue he edited, disparaging "the sensuous cynicism of Mr. Bowles, who seems to have wandered through the California 'greenwood' . . . with an equal facility for moralizing over a wounded dear 'i' the forest,' or expatiating upon the juiciness of a haunch from the same animal, carried about, cold, wrapped up in a copy of the *Springfield Republican*."[30] Still, the *Republican* hailed Harte's rising star in the western firmament upon his resignation from the *Overland* in January 1871—"We have no magazine editor on the Atlantic coast, perhaps, who could have done for the Overland what its first editor did"[31]—and the paper dutifully traced his journey across the continent to Boston the next month, a trip W. D. Howells years later compared to "the progress of a prince, in the universal attention and interest which met and followed it."[32] Who could have guessed that, removed from the sources of his inspiration, Harte would soon exhaust both his Eastern welcome and the rich vein of Western material he had been working?

BIBLIOGRAPHICAL NOTE

Because they were not published in California but in Massachusetts, the vast majority of these letters to the *Christian Register* and *Springfield Republican* have hitherto been lost to scholarship. George R. Stewart, Jr., listed none of them in his standard "Bibliography of the Writings of Bret Harte in the Magazines and Newspapers of California 1857–1871," the most comprehensive bibliography of Harte's work published to date.[33] Nevertheless, Stewart unearthed some of the pieces in the late 1920s as he researched Harte's life. He examined a cache of clippings from the *Republican* the author apparently left with his sister when he moved east in 1871 and which, in 1928, was still in the possession of Harte's aged niece in Berkeley. In 1930, Stewart "completed" the collection, or so he thought, by scanning the files of the *Republican*. In 1951, then, Stewart and Edwin Fussell reprinted the first eleven articles Harte sent the paper in a chapbook edition of 400 copies issued by the Book Club of California under the title

San Francisco in 1866.[34] Incredibly, however, this volume failed to include—because Stewart had failed to locate—any of the eight essays Harte wrote for the *Republican*, after nearly a five-month hiatus, in 1867. Similarly, Stewart was familiar with some, but not all, of Harte's contributions to the *Register*. He briefly mentioned two of them in his 1931 biography of Harte, for example.[35] From all indications, however, he did not search the *Register* carefully, perhaps because back copies of the paper are rare. Stewart overlooked letters 18 and 35, it seems, else he would have incorporated Harte's comments on Mark Twain in these letters into a piece he published in *American Literature* in 1941. Instead, he merely cited in this article the final paragraph of letter 25.[36] Nor was Stewart aware of the essays Harte wrote for the *Register* in 1867; in fact, he mistakenly claimed in his biography that by the end of 1866 "Harte had ceased to contribute to either" the *Republican* or *Register*.[37] In short, most of these pieces have long been lost in a bibliographical blindspot, and twenty-six of the thirty-seven are reprinted here for the first time since their original publication in 1866–67.

I have silently corrected obvious typographical errors in the printed texts, though I have not tried to regularize Harte's often idiosyncratic spelling and punctuation. I am grateful to Sibylle Zemitis of the California State Library and my colleague Scott Sanders for their help in the preparation of this volume.

Notes

1. King to Fields, 31 January 1862. Quoted by permission of the Huntington Library, San Marino, California.

2. [T. Starr] K[ing], "Letter from San Francisco," *Boston Transcript*, 7 November 1862, 2:3; rpt. in the *Christian Register*, 15 November 1862, p. 181.

3. Bradford A. Booth, "Unpublished Letters of Bret Harte," *American Literature* 16 (May 1944): 133.

4. *Stories and Poems and Other Uncollected Writings of Bret Harte*, ed. C. M. Kozlay (Boston and New York: Houghton Mifflin, 1914), pp. 310–311; Harte, *Complete Poetical Works* (Boston and New York: Houghton Mifflin, 1902), pp. 13, 16. "Relieving Guard" also appeared in the *Boston Transcript*, 11 April 1864, 1:4; and "At the Sepulchre" in the *Boston Transcript*, 21 November 1864, 4:3.

5. George R. Stewart, Jr., *Bret Harte: Argonaut and Exile* (Boston and New York: Houghton Mifflin, 1931), pp. 87–88.

6. Charles W. Wendte, *Thomas Starr King: Patriot and Preacher* (Boston: Beacon Press, 1921), p. 165; Stewart, *Bret Harte*, p. 140.

7. Stewart, *Bret Harte*, p. 115.

8. C. H. W[ebb], "The Pacific Coast," *New York Times*, 15 February 1866, 3:3–5; "Letter from San Francisco," *Sacramento Union*, 8 December 1865, 3:3–4; 15 December 1865, 3:3; Stewart, *Bret Harte*, p. 134.

9. Harte to Webb, 18 October 1866. Quoted by permission of the Bancroft Library, University of California, Berkeley, California.

10. *Mark Twain's Letters 1853–1866*, ed. Edgar M. Branch *et al.* (Berkeley: University of California Press, 1988), p. 328.

11. Harte to Sawyer, 18 December 1866. Quoted by permission of the Massachusetts Historical Society, Boston, Massachusetts.

12. I have omitted from this collection Harte's early article "Unitarian Conference in California," which appeared in the *Christian Register* for 21 April 1866. This article consists largely of excerpted resolutions and speeches that Harte recorded at the behest of the editor and is thus different in kind from the other letters in this correspondence.

13. H[oratio] S[tebbins], "The Great San Francisco Earthquake," *Springfield Republican*, 13 November 1865, 2:5.

14. William Bross, "An Overland Journey," *Chicago Tribune*, 16 August 1865, 2:3; Samuel Bowles, *Across the Continent* (New York: Hurd and Houghton, 1865), pp. 321, 332.

15. Stewart, *Bret Harte*, p. 146.

16. "New Publications," San Francisco *Evening Bulletin*, 7 February 1866, 1:1; rpt. "'Across the Continent' in California," *Springfield Republican*, 7 March 1866, 1:3. The *Bulletin* also described Harte as "the accomplished San Francisco correspondent of the Springfield (Mass.) *Republican*" and excerpted letter 22 in its columns ("California Watering Places," 10 January 1867, 5:4).

17. Harte to Bowles, 9 August 1867. Quoted by permission of the Bancroft Library, University of California, Berkeley, California. Harte also commended the "thoughtful analysis" of Bowles's book in the *Overland Monthly*, 3 (August 1869), 193–194.

18. "To the Oldest Man," *Springfield Republican*, 26 September 1866, 2:2.

19. "Books, Authors and Art," *Springfield Republican*, 16 January 1867, 4:3.

20. *Springfield Republican*, 22 May 1867, 1:6.

21. John Paul [pseudo.], "Letter from New York," *Springfield Republican*, 29 May 1867, 4:4.

22. Harte to Bowles, 9 August 1867. Quoted by permission of the Bancroft Library, University of California, Berkeley, California.

23. T. M., "From California," *Springfield Republican*, 18 December 1867, 2:4–5.

24. "The Magazines Once More," *Springfield Republican*, 9 September 1868, 2:2.

25. "The Luck of Roaring Camp," *Springfield Republican*, 12 September 1868, 6:1–3; "Two Rising Monthlies," *Springfield Republican*, 30 September 1868, 2:2.

26. See, for example, the *Springfield Republican* for the following dates: 9 June 1869, 2:2; 29 December 1869, 2:2; 4 April 1870, 2:3; 3 May 1870, 2:1; 4 July 1870, 2:1–2; 5 September 1870, 2:3.

27. "The Outcasts of Poker Flat," 1 February 1869, 6:1–3; "Miggles," 14 June 1869, 6:1–3; "Tennessee's Partner," 9 October 1869, 6:1–3; "Mr. Thompson's Prodigal," 2 July 1870, 6:1–3; and "Plain Language from Truthful James," 31 August 1870, 7:6. The paper also reprinted Harte's poems "Dickens in Camp," 4 July 1870, 6:2; "Further Language from Truthful James," 31 December 1870, 7:6; and "The Hawk's Nest," 20 March 1871, 6:1.

28. "Mr. Harte's Sketches," *Springfield Republican*, 25 April 1870, 2:1–2; "Bret Harte's Poems," *Springfield Republican*, 26 December 1870, 2:2.

29. *Springfield Republican*, 25 April 1870, 2:2.

30. "Current Literature," *Overland Monthly*, 6 (February 1871), 192.

31. *Springfield Republican*, 20 March 1871, 2:4; 3 April 1871, 2:1; 15 February 1871, 2:1–2 and 4:1; 17 February 1871, 4:1.

32. W. D. Howells, *Literary Friends and Acquaintance* (New York: Harpers, 1900), p. 290.

33. *University of California Publications in English* 3 (1933): 119–70.

34. (San Francisco: Book Club of California, 1951), pp. vi and *passim*.

35. Stewart, *Bret Harte*, pp. 145, 151.

36. "Bret Harte Upon Mark Twain," *American Literature* 13 (November 1941): 263–64.

37. Stewart, *Bret Harte*, p. 145.

The First Unitarian Church of San Francisco and Tomb of T. Starr King, described in letters 3 and 37. (Reprinted from C. W. Wendte, Thomas Starr King: Patriot and Preacher *[Boston: Beacon, 1921])*

Thomas Starr King circa 1864. (Reprinted from Wendte, Thomas Starr King)

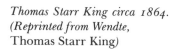

Telegraph Hill in 1865. (Photo by T. E. Hecht. Courtesy of Bancroft Library, University of California)

Maguire's Opera House where Edwin Forrest performed (letter 9) and Mark Twain delivered his first lecture (letter 25). (Photo by T. E. Hecht. Courtesy of Bancroft Library, University of California)

Pine and Montgomery Streets in 1865. (Photo by T. E. Hecht. Courtesy of Bancroft Library, University of California)

The Occidental Hotel, where Queen Emma registered (letter 24). (Photo by T. E. Hecht. Courtesy of Bancroft Library, University of California)

LETTER 1

Christian Register, 17 February 1866

[From our Regular Correspondent.]

CALIFORNIA.

San Francisco, Jan. 18, 1866.

The annual renting of pews in the Geary Street Unitarian Church (Rev. Mr. Stebbins's) took place on the 15th ult. The rain pretermitted somewhat its fury, and the evening was clear and starlight. The church was comfortably filled with ladies and gentlemen—an attendance about as large as the average Sunday congregation of other churches. The bidding was spirited, and showed no falling off in the zeal of parishioners or in the sympathizing interest of the many strangers who attend this place of worship. The first choice of pews brought a premium of $500, (gold); the second, $400 (gold); the third, fourth, and fifth, each, $350 (gold); one of them being knocked down to Moses Ellis, Esq., now bodily in Boston, but in spirit, at least, represented in the church where he so long worshipped. The total amount of the premium thus collected was—translated into the language of your currency—$12,000. The total rental of the pews, in the same familiar medium, $17,000, the average plate contributions are $6,300, making a total revenue per annum of $35,300.

It seems hard to measure spiritual results by dollars and cents, but in this material community the figures I have just quoted indicate more plainly than any rhetoric I could use, the value set upon Liberal Christianity on this coast, as well as the popular estimate of the labors of our earnest and eloquent pastor. The personal compliment to him, a few months ago, took the shape of $4,000 (gold). The same fine barbarian instincts, which induce the natives a little further west to load their missionary with oranges and breadfruit, perhaps found expression in the manner shown above. But I cannot help thinking that the gift honored both recipient and giver. It was a tacit recognition of good through the popular currency—a legal tender, valuable chiefly as the promise of something better in deposit.

Let not anything here written be construed into an intimation that the prosperity of Liberal Christianity here would at present justify the addition of another minister and another parish. The rumor which has reverberated to these shores that a call has been already given, is entirely without foundation. The time is not yet. The association is not large enough to be divided without weakening. There is need of centralization and concentration rather than scattered or sporadic effort. It is true that the duties of a pastor here are onerous and incessant; how onerous, how incessant let the sacrifice of Thomas Starr King, whose precious life-chords snapped under the tension of four years' ceaseless toil, too plainly testify. It is true that already the broad frame and sturdy Northern physique of our present energetic shepherd is beginning to show as plainly the wearisome, distracting and exacting duties of his charge. Yet he feels, as we all do, the necessity of a continued and familiar personality in the church, and would rather, I think, sink beneath his burthen, than suffer any harm to come to the society through a division of its present harmonious forces. The Rev. Mr. Ames, who has won many friends by the sweetness and flavor of a consecrated nature and a broad range of tender sympathies, occasionally relieves Mr. Stebbins in his pulpit duties, and is always welcome. During the illness of that gentleman, Mr. Ames labored faithfully and ardently in his stead. It is perhaps owing to this timely rest that Mr. Stebbins is quietly recovering his pristine vigor, which for the past month had been dimmed by fever and cold.

The annual church meeting, held on the 16th, resulted in the re-election of Robert B. Swain as moderator, and a member of the old board. Every one interested in the welfare of the society and the Liberal cause will be glad to hear that this quiet, blue-eyed man, who has presided over the practical destinies of the church since 1856, and yet found time to stand at the head of benevolent societies and act as the impelling life and energy of all movements of reform and philanthropy, by consenting to take the helm,—has insured the material success of the society for another year. The dear friend and fellow-laborer of Mr King, the historian of his life and sacrifice, it is not to be wondered that his report was touching, tender and graceful in its allusions to the past, or effective in its exhortations to the society to respect the last wishes of their beloved pastor.   H.

LETTER 2

Christian Register, 24 February 1866

[From our Regular Correspondent.]

CALIFORNIA.

San Francisco, Jan. 18, 1866.

An interval in one of those monotonous deluges which indicate our California winter, brought us some compensation the other day in a rare and beautiful spectacle. As the clouds lifted we saw the mountains of Contra Costa and the low hills which encompass our city glittering with freshly fallen *snow*. San Francisco gazed and wondered; the oldest inhabitants had never seen the like. Here was the familiar face of Monte del Diablo masquerading beneath a white domino; Mission Peak had borrowed for the occasion the mantle of Shasta. Yet the scene was characteristic. The slopes of the hills were green with budding grasses, and the snow-line encroached no further along the declivity than does the foam that casts a long swinging wave. The glow of spring and the rigor of winter were divided by a boundary as accurately defined as the edges of our two solitary seasons. There was no intermediate or transitive state.

Many climbed the steeper grades of the city to view this strange prospect, rimmed with frigid color. It was the livery of spring turned up with winter. The warm, moist earth beneath their feet was quick with the life of daisies and butter-cups, for vegetation in this prolific soil never seems to utterly die, but rather to be buried under the ashes of the dead summer, which pelting storms beat away, and a thousand tiny bayonets are always ready to spring out when the rain beats its "long roll" over their heads. The sun shone brightly and would have shone warmly; but the wind, blowing over the white and silent peaks beyond, was "nipping and eager," and San Francisco for the first time felt the severity of a winter's chill. Not but that we suffer from cold quite as sensibly as you do; but our sensitiveness does not result from any thermometrical phenomena: rather from some predisposing quality in the dry atmosphere, some law superior to isothermal lines. Yet we gazed longingly toward the snow-fields. Visions of snow-balling and sleigh-riding, of blue smoke curling from white-capped chimneys and indicating genial firesides below and the thousand fascinating associations of an Eastern winter swam before our eyes. For we do not change our allegiance with change of sky any more now than in the days when that truthful sentiment was first written. Scratch the most blatant Californian and you will find an Eastern man beneath. His loyalty is only an incrustation. Howbeit, the visions quickly vanished; the wind veered again to the stormy southwest, the clouds gathered and once more hid the distant hills, and when the sun again shone the snow was gone, and our airy castles, based on that uncertain foundation, had dissolved, like Prospero's "unsubstantial pageant." Since then we have had one or two exceptional days of clear weather; but as a general thing our changes have been limited to mist and rain, rain and mist, rain with and without hail, rain with and without wind, but always with a well-defined basis of rain. If you find me tedious on this topic remember how much has been written concerning our climate and yet, judging from the expectations of new comers, how little understood.

We are just now suffering from reaction after the holidays. Christmas came and went to the sound of toy drums and a peculiar kind of trumpet, evidently a local invention, as it had all the bleakness of a San Francisco landscape in its blare. The treeless city was invaded by Christmas evergreens,—tall young pines and firs from the nearest mountains, decked with colored gew-gaws, as though Birnam Wood had come to Dunsinane and brought its things. Christmas and New Years are fully observed; generous giving marked the first, overflowing hospitality the second; for we lack not the barbaric virtues. On Christmas day the churches were pretty well attended. At the Willows, a suburban resort, there was a bull-fight; but, whether intended as a seasonable and delicate compliment to the founders of this blessed city of St. Francis of Assisi, and looked upon by their descendants as a religious observance, I cannot say. Probably we have outgrown the worship but not the amusements of our Catholic pioneers.   H.

Letter 3

Christian Register, 14 April 1866

[From our Regular Correspondent.]

CALIFORNIA.

San Francisco, March 9, 1866.

Sunday, the 4th day of March, 1866, was the second anniversary of the death of Thomas Starr King. The day was bright and beautiful as that on which, two years ago, his dying eyes closed so trustfully. The modest little tomb wherein his ashes lie, which stands in the quadrangle beside his church, was tenderly decked with flowers; wreaths of Egyptian lilies hung from its coped roof, festoons of fresh violets half hid the scarlet letters of the old English inscription, and the words "In Memoriam" bloomed in perennial *immortelles* around its base. It was as though Spring, precocious and prodigal as she is in this strange climate, had exhausted her vocabulary to write his epitaph. The church itself, his truer monument, was thronged with a multitude to whom his memory was precious, and from the pulpit his presence had consecrated, the argument of an eloquent discourse upon the "Divine Nature in Humanity" was illustrated by a tender tribute to his memory. Long after the service was over the people lingered in groups beside the railing which encloses his tomb. There was, perhaps, a consistency in the selection of its site, which answers any objection which might be raised to the simplicity and plainness of the tomb itself. It is a compromise between the civic monument which San Francisco wanted to raise, and the ecclesiastical mural tablet which it was first intended should grace the church. The sound of passing footsteps, and the bustle and life of a great thoroughfare, reach you as you stand beside it, and suggest the humanity of which he was a true apostle. The larger week-day congregations of all sects and creeds, who knew and loved him, can here join freely in reverence and worship at his tomb. For his broad, Catholic spirit passed even the liberal boundaries of his own church, which stands near enough to attest his vocation, but even whose informal walls do not enclose the mute pulpit from which the greatest lesson of his life is preached.

The Rev. Mr. Ames is in Sacramento. The Rev. Mr. Stone, of your city, has arrived, and preaches his first sermon in San Francisco tomorrow at Dr. Lacey's church.

With the President's veto the topic of excited comment and a subject of vital importance to all interested in the moral results of our late national struggle, you can readily believe that the pulpit, which during the war never dodged the discussion of any question, political or secular, which involved the sacred principles of right and truth, did not now shrink from free and candid expressions. On the Sunday following the reception of the telegraphic news, Mr. Stebbins made the all-absorbing topic the theme of his morning's discourse. It was earnest, without being partisan; politic without weakness. While he avowed his sympathy with those principles which it was feared were threatened by the veto, he did not think this was an occasion to vindicate them. Taking his text from Romans 13,i: "The powers that be are ordained of God," he deprecated hasty condemnation of our rulers, and called to mind how easily evil was believed of public officers,—how great the lack of confidence in public men. He believed that no amount of public trust or service would shield a man from the imputation of the basest motives, if in any way he disappointed his constituency, or acted with a high, noble sense of public duty beyond the lines of ordinary partisanship. "The conception of government," said Mr. Stebbins, "as a merely mundane thing, as a human contrivance, that law originates with the people, if not strongly offset by the nobler truth that all government is divine order through human media, naturally runs to a low plane of thinking and acting concerning the State." He begged his hearers to exercise carefulness in eliciting the facts of the question; he himself would not make up his mind nor would he discuss just then the merits of the bill or veto with our present imperfect information. He thought the President's speech gave more cause for alarm than the veto, in its exhibition of wilfulness, vindictiveness, narrowness and want of dignity; but it was unfair to judge of the merits of the veto from that. He did not despair, even in the worst. He enumerated many facts, which should be especially considered as throwing more or less light on the gloom and present obscurity which surrounded the subject, and paid

the following tribute to the wisdom and integrity of Mr. Seward, which
I am tempted to give in his own language:—

"There is an important consideration included within the spirit
of these remarks, which I cannot neglect. Able and patriotic
men, who have had the confidence of the American people, and
who have rendered unspeakable service to the country and mankind, appear to be somewhat divided. For instance, the Secretary
of State approves the President's course; the Chairman of the
Finance Committee disapproves it. What strikes me as one of the
symptoms of opinion, is the readiness with which we affirm that
the Secretary has abandoned a cause for which he has suffered
even death itself. No fact of distinguished and unparalleled service has a moment's weight as against a mind of discontent. About
a year ago, when the untimely death of the President spread
gloom over the land, and we all feared that the life of the Secretary was involved in those awful deeds of cowardice, with what
trembling emotions we all expressed our gratitude that he was
spared, and our hope that his life might be precious in the sight
of heaven.

"O, beautiful sentiment of sorrow! Endearing grace of moral
love! Gratitude and prayer of a trusting people! Is this all swept
away in the gust of a momentary disappointment? You all remember the wild enthusiasm of the country, at the capture of
two distinguished rebels from an English mail steamer. A public opinion based on pride and exaltation, sprang up in a night
like Aladdin's castle. Grave judges of supreme courts, came down
from their judicial dignities and in popular harangue, approved
on principles of law, the conduct of the American officer. Public declaimers throughout the land, fanned the flame of opinion
which flashed from East to West, casting its gleam on the midnight clouds of war. The Secretary knew that all that was wrong.
With matchless power of comprehension, and marvellous sweep
of diplomatic discourse, he dissolved that public opinion, and
took down the castle of glass without a break. Is consummate
ability, supreme caution, and moral courage, verging on audacity,
to be counted of no worth, and to be swept away at every whisper
of the receding tide of the lower politics? It is a sad and sorry
criticism on our public virtue. We treat it as if it were a myth.
I affirm that the readiness—the matter-of-course way in which
we account for the conduct of public men by their dishonesty is

nothing less than shocking. If a man by honorable conduct and great usefulness in any department of the government, has retained a place through many vicissitudes, we charge him with time-serving; and if, by any sagacity of statesmanship, he applies his principles to new conditions, we charge him with abandoning those principles." H.

LETTER 4

Christian Register, 28 April 1866

[From our Regular Correspondent.]

CALIFORNIA.

San Francisco, March, 1866.

The winter's rains are not yet over, although spring arrived a month ago, and we have even been treated to those ferocious zephyrs, known as "summer winds." The California spring is, in fact, unlike any other season. It does not change into summer, neither is it perennial; its budding youth never develops into maturity and fruition, but is protracted throughout the year in a kind of withered, unprofitable virginity that gets to be very shrill and shrewish toward the close. When it ends finally, it does not fade away with the hectic flush and consumptive beauty of an Eastern autumn; it dies of atrophy with all the hippocratic signs of dissolution—cavernous, sunken, rigid, colorless and cold. If I am somewhat voluble on this subject and use strong figures it is because I feel strongly. Having tried for twelve years to appreciate this remarkable climate, I am anxious to give some good reason for my failure. The country is youthful and ambitious, and nature has not yet completely adjusted herself to new conditions. She offers grandeur, sublimity and picturesqueness, and delights in heroic attitudes before the tourists, but of purely bucolic and pastoral comfort she knows nothing. She offers you quantity instead of quality— opulence in place of refinement. The same law she obeys in producing monstrous cabbages and gigantic trees is shown throughout the details of her landscape. If she has to make a mountain it is something stupendous; if a valley, it is a perpendicular chasm of several thousand feet, like the Yo Semite; if she has even to cover a field with flowers, it is done so extravagantly that the scentless blossoms seem to have been furnished by contract. Her rains are deluges—her droughts are six months long. What she loses in delicacy she makes up in fibre—whether it be strawberries that look as if they had been arrested on their way to become pine-apples, or a field of wild oats, whose every stalk is a miracle of size, but whose general effect is most unpastoral and unmeadow-like. The effect on the inhabitants may be readily conceived. We have *ranchos* instead of farms, *vaqueros* for milk-maids; the "neat-handed Phillis" is apt to be a Chinaman, and our gentle shepherds are swarthy looking Mexicans.

Speaking of Chinamen reminds me that the Chinese New Year may be now regularly counted among our San Francisco anniversaries—a week in February being devoted to the explosion of fire crackers in the upper part of Sacramento street and along the classic shades of Dupont and Kearney streets where these people have their habitations. Most of the Chinese merchants kept open house this year, and received their countrymen and a few select "outside barbarians." The temples, rich in barbaric gilding and color, and unspeakably noisesome and filthy, were open and the usual ceremonies performed. As the only clear ideas I have of Buddha are that his attributes are best expressed in noise and dirt, I am afraid I could not give you a fair or intelligible idea of their devotions. For a nation with such a tremendous history they impress you but feebly. The modern Chinese gives you no more idea of Confucius than the modern Greek gives you of Socrates. But they make peaceable citizens and I think, yield to our civilization here, slowly but surely. I do not participate in Prof. Draper's fears about their introducing polygamy on this coast in conjunction with the Mormons, at least for some years. Just now the balance of immorality seems to be the other way and sympathy should obtain for the Chinese. As an individual, John Chinaman is generally honest, painstaking, simple and industrious. He makes a good servant, and like Malvolio is "sad and civil." In fact, the expression of the Chinese face in the aggregate, is neither cheerful nor happy. There is an abiding consciousness of degradation—a secret pain of self-humiliation visible in the lines of the mouth and eye. Whether this is a modified expression of Eastern gravity, or whether it is the effect of the dread Valley of the Shadow of the Drug, through which they are so often straying, I cannot say. They seldom smile, and their laughter is of such an extraordinary and sardonic quality—so purely a mechanical spasm, quite independent of any mirthful attribute, that your own mirth is seldom provoked by their's. Their ideas of humor are more or less vague; at their theatres they laugh—sardonically of course—at the frequent decapitations and murders which enliven the play, but the hero, after an agonizing death, quietly walks off the stage without exciting any ridicule. They are patient under abuse, and that patience, I am ashamed to say, they have to exercise continually in California.   H.

LETTER 5

Springfield Republican, 5 May 1866
Springfield Weekly Republican, 12 May 1866

FROM CALIFORNIA.

The Last Earthquake—The Social, Moral and Commercial Influences of Earthquakes—The Legislature and Its Corruptions—The Chinese Question and Mr Burlingame—Is the California Sun Hot?

[From Our Special Correspondent.]

San Francisco, April 5, 1866.

The earthquake which visited this coast on the 26th ult., and of which you have probably been informed by telegraph, was, on the whole, a rather good-humored affair. It was more like a hospitable exhibition of California productions to our latest guests, Messrs Van Valkenburgh, Stone and Burlingame, than anything else, and lacked the peculiar *animus* and decided malevolence of the shock of October last. That was a trespass with assault and battery superadded.

The late shock was felt generally throughout the state, although the interior papers, with provincial jealousy, intimate that it was more severe in San Francisco than elsewhere, and that the metropolis aggrandized even this impartial convulsion as she does everything else. It exhibited the usual phenomena which have become familiar to us without losing their awe-inspiring qualities. There was the premonitory thrill, followed by an interval of awful suspense; the ominous rumble and rattle; the shock in its different manifestations of rolling, bumping, swaying or jolting, and the succeeding hush, broken at last by anxious voices, shuffling feet, barking of dogs, neighing of horses and crowing of cocks. At such times the streets are filled with people narrowly inspecting the walls and cornices of the houses they have just quitted, or excitedly comparing their experiences. Above all this bustle and confusion the clear blue of a Californian sky demurely arches, and a bright unclouded sun looks good-humoredly down. Finding, perhaps, that nature does not generally participate in the convulsion, people begin to smile and joke, the color returns to blanched cheeks, business is resumed, and the restless microcosm of life and labor goes on undisturbed until another shock shall disintegrate it.

Familiarity with earthquakes does not beget contempt—there is surprising freshness and novelty in each new alarm—and although Californians are not inclined to confess timidity, and although some affect to treat these phenomena in the light of a gigantic practical joke, it may be noted that for an hour or two after a shock, out-of-door exercise and promenading become fashionable and popular, and the influx of passengers in the streets is remarkable large. An earthquake is the one touch of nature that makes the whole world kin. The slightest shock is sufficient to overthrow the artificial barriers of society. Mistress and maid faint in each other's arms. "Washoe" in his gilded palace and Pat in his shanty forsake their respective habitations to find safety in the democratic thoroughfare.

In spite of the fears of alarmists, I do not think that the prosperity and future of California is disturbed by these shocks, and I believe that there is more danger to be apprehended from the concealment of facts, or the tacit silence of the public press on this topic, than in the free and open discussion of the subject and speculation for the future. Only weak walls and weaker principles and theories have thus far been overthrown, and earthquakes have been beneficial in so far as they have tested the fealty of Californians to their adopted state. Those who have been the most blatant and vulgar in their praises of the country, who have extolled even its faults and imperfections; who have indulged in retrospective longings for a return of "'49 and '50" and their attendant barbarisms as the acme of California prosperity —the very parvenus of a parvenu civilization—are now boisterous in their defection and alarming in their prophesies for the future. On the other hand, those who have been generally termed "growlers;" who have exposed the absurdity of extolling the climate and scenery above all others; who have hinted that long dry summers and wet winters are not picturesque; are ready and willing to accept earthquakes, drouths and inundations as the not-too-exorbitant price that must be paid for a practical, healthy and labor-saving climate and a fruitful and aurif-erous soil. Physical disturbances are the least dangers that threaten our prosperity; we have passed through ordeals more serious than the earthquake shock. Ruffianism, brigandage, chivalry, gambling, scan-dalous legislation, lynch law, and extravagant speculation have in turn retarded our progress. The pistol and knife, drunkenness and de-bauchery, have claimed more victims than ever pestilence, flood or volcanic throe.

If common report and the charges of the public press are to be be-lieved, the Legislature, which has just adjourned, was preeminently unscrupulous and obnoxious even for this country of reckless legis-lation. Bribes were freely accepted; it is alleged that shamefully ex-travagant bills were passed for a consideration; and in one instance advantage was taken of the popularity of the Pacific railroad—that subject upon which Californians are so eloquent and so inactive—to pass a kind of railroad bill, whose only apparent object was to benefit a few individuals at the public expense. This bill passed both houses, but was providentially vetoed by the governor. It would have been well had he also vetoed another bill, to raise the already high fares on the city railroads, which has become a law. But the people are too grateful to their executive for estopping the larger swindle to grumble about this lesser though equally unprincipled extortion. So reckless had legislation become, that the news of adjournment was received in this city with expressions of joy and relief. I know of several instances, where financial enterprises were purposely delayed by their projectors until the possibility of sinister legislative interference had passed, and security in vested capital was restored. Poor men were ousted from established privileges and vocations by franchises passed over their heads to a few favored capitalists. Lawless speculation ruled; legitimate enterprise was checked, and business was in a measure suspended.

Of course a certain California exaggeration overlies these general charges against our lawgivers. It must be remembered, to their credit, that they recently cited the editor of a violently radical and aggressive sheet—who, I think, aspires to be the Marat of some sanguinary California revolution, and whose paper, during the excitement that followed Lincoln's assassination, lacked only ability to complete its resemblance to *Ami du Peuple*—to appear and substantiate certain charges of corruption against them, and failing to get an answer, committed him for contempt. But the unwise Solons kept him in prison so long that, without vindicating their own honor, they narrowly escaped elevating their victim to the glory of martyrdom. These facts taken in conjunction with another, viz., that the general tone and *motif* of California civilization and journalism is *aggressive*—that California wit is personal and epithetic—that a story that does not affect the reputation or respectability of some prominent man loses half its point,—that the conventional expression of a joke is "to have a good thing *on* such and such a one," should have due weight in determining the amount of exaggeration in these wholesale accusations.

Our Chinese question, which even Prof Draper treats with serious concern, was a few days ago intelligently, though informally, discussed in this city. A dinner was given to Messrs Van Valkenburgh and Burlingame by C. W. Brooks, Esq., the Japanese commercial agent, and a number of prominent and able representative men met and discussed the different bearings and aspects of our relations to Cathay and her people. The tone of thought and sentiment was liberal, farseeing, broad and catholic, and a policy consistent with this liberality was unanimously agreed upon as the policy of California in her attitude to Asiatic civilization at home or abroad. Although this gathering was informal and social, these expressions were significant and prophetic, coming from men of authority and weight. Commerce, law and government were represented at the board, and liberal Christianity, in the presence of Rev Horatio Stebbins, lent a moral and missionary importance to the occasion.

We are enjoying the early bloom of our precocious but never-maturing spring. March reversed the usual proverb, and went out with a lion-like tempestuousness. But the rule of contraries obtains in this climate; our summers are cold and disagreeable; our winters are warm and genial. Apropos, there seems to be a question of fact between the New York Nation and the San Francisco correspondent of the New York Times touching the "fervor" of the California sun. The Nation,

I believe, claims the correctness of this epithet; the Times correspondent denies that the sun is at all hot. My observation coincides with the Nation as to temperature, but I should hardly apply the epithet applied by the Nation, or conveyed by the context in its relation to "erotic poetry." The sun is hot, but its beams are modified by a dry atmosphere to the chastity of Diana. It does not provoke the dreamy, sensuous languor of the tropics. Miss Ophelia might have walked in it without exposing herself to the dangers hinted at by Hamlet; it produces no poetry, erotic or otherwise; it is the *fornax* or furnace heat, and not the animated glow of vitality.   F.B.H.

LETTER 6

Christian Register, 19 May 1866

[From our Regular Correspondent.]

CALIFORNIA.

San Francisco, April 10, 1866.

Of the fifty houses of public worship in San Francisco, there is but one that has a history older than ten or twelve years, or around whose walls the associations of past generations still cling. It is the church of the Mission Dolores. It was dedicated in 1776, and is as old as the Republic. When Hancock and Adams, on the eastern shore of the continent, were watching by the cradle of the young confederation, Father Francisco Palou and Father Benito Cambon founded this Mission to perpetuate and extend the power and dominion of the holy church. That was ninety years ago, and the Mission-church stands where it did, crumbling and time-worn, forgotten in the Republic that has crossed the continent to absorb it.

As a real bit of antiquity in this land of new formations, new buildings, and creatures of yesterday, I have often thought that the old *adobe* chapel should be protected by legislative enactment from disturbance or removal. But within the last year it has been plastered and stuccoed—"restored," I believe they call it—so that nothing of the old exterior remains but its contour, while every stroke of the vandal's trowel and brush has blotted out and erased some old association. I remember, two years ago at this season, looking at the chapel,— its ragged senility in high contrast with the dapper spring sunshine, its two gouty pillars, with the plaster dropping off like tattered bandages, its rayless windows, the leperspots on its whitewashed wall eating through to the dark *adobe*, and giving the old mendicant but a few years longer to sit by the wayside and ask alms in the names of the blessed saints. Even there the vicinity was haunted with a prophecy of the coming change. The shriek of the locomotive discorded with the Angelus bell. An Episcopal church of a green Gothic type, with deceitful buttresses of Oregon pine, mocked its hoary age with imitation, and supplanted it with a sham. Even the old rural accessories, the market-gardens and nurseries, that once gathered about its walls, and resisted civic encroachment, were passing away. A few small *adobe* buildings, with tiled roofs, like longitudinal strips of cinnamon, and walled enclosures sacredly guarding a few strips of hide, still stood there; but I missed their tenants,—the half-reclaimed Mexican, whose respectability stopped at his waist, and whose red sash under his vest was the utter undoing of his black broadcloth. I missed also the female of his species,—the swarthy-faced, black-haired women, whose dresses always appeared unseasonable in texture and pattern, and whose manner of wearing a shawl was a terrible awakening from the poetic dream of the Spanish mantilla. Traces of another nationality were visible. The Irish railroad-laborer had builded his cabin near the chapel, and smoked his pipe in the *posada*.

As I lingered beside the old church yesterday, I noticed many changes which seemed to indicate that my prophecies of two years ago were in a fair way to become realized. There was something ominous in its new coat of whitewash, as if progress had licked it over previous to swallowing it completely. At the very gates of the temple—in the place of those "who sell doves for sacrifice"—a vender of mechanical spiders had halted with his unhallowed wares. Even the old padre— last type of the old missionary and descendant of the good Junipero —I could not find; in his stead a light-haired Celt was reading the lesson from a Vulgate that seemed singularly replete with double r's. Gentle priest, in thy r-isms be the sins of the stranger and heretic remembered!

I opened a little gate and entered the Mission church-yard. The chronicle tells me that the first interment here took place in 1776. But I have forgotten if the chronicle gives the name of the worthy pioneer; and as I stood there, perhaps over his unrecorded dust, I wondered if his gentle soul was vexed that he had been crowded out of recognition by the parvenu dead of yesterday. There was little change here, though the graves lay close together. A willow tree growing beside the wall had burst in tufted plumes in the fullness of spring. The tall grass-blades over each mound showed an ominous quickening of the soil below. The cemetery of Lone Mountain aggrandizes the dead of the metropolis; but I can fancy that it would be pleasanter to lie here than in that bleak mountain to the seaward, where distracting winds continually bring the strife and turmoil of the ocean. The Mission hills lovingly embrace the little graveyard, and break the summer gales. The decorative taste here, too, is less ostentatious. The foreign flavor is strong; there are many French inscriptions. Here are the never-fading garlands of *immortelles*, with their sepulchral spice; here are little cheap medallions of pewter, with the adornment of three palpable black tears, that would look like the tray of clubs, but that the simple humility of the inscription counterbalances all sense of the ridiculous. Here are children's graves, with guardian angels of awful specific gravity; but here, too, is the quiet pathos of the little one's toys in a glass case beside them. Here are the average quantity of execrable original verses; but I noticed one stanza over a sailor's grave that was striking and original, for it expressed a hope of salvation through the "Lord High Admiral Christ!" Over the foreign graves there was a notable lack of Scriptural quotation and formulæ, and a gain, if I may say it, of humanity and tenderness. I cannot help thinking that it is a fault of our religion to make too much of a practical point on this occasion, and we are too apt to hastily crowd a whole life of omission with this culminating expression of faith. Hence, when I see the grey *immortelles* crowning a tombstone, I know I shall find the mysteries of the resurrection taught rather in symbol than recitation of creed, and only the love and humanity taught in His new commandment shown on the graven stone. But "they manage these things better in France."

During my ramble the sun had been steadily climbing the brown wall of the church, and the air seemed to grow cold and raw as the day wore on. The afternoon fogs were stealing in noiseless marches through the gaps of the hills, or soothing the wind-buffetted faces of the headlands. The bright green died out of the grass, and the rich bronze came down from the wall. The willow tree seemed half-inclined to doff its plumes as premature, and wore the air of a violated trust; for, in this locality, two hours in the afternoon is sufficient to change the whole aspect of nature. The spice of *immortelles* mingled with the incense that stole through the open window. Within, the barbaric gilt and coloring looked cheap and cold in that searching air; by that light the church was decidedly old and ugly, and as I turned away I could not help wondering whether the pious founders, if they ever revisited the scenes of their former labors, in their larger comprehensions, viewed with regret the impending change, or mourned over the day when the Mission Dolores shall appropriately come to grief.   H.

LETTER 7

Springfield Republican, 26 May 1866
Springfield Weekly Republican, 2 June 1866

FROM CALIFORNIA.

The Nitro-Glycerine Explosion at San Francisco—Its Physical and Moral
Features—The Dead and the Living.

[From Our Special Correspondent.]

San Francisco, April 20, 1866.

The terrible explosion at Wells, Fargo & Co.'s building in this city on the 16th inst., which suddenly dashed out the life and cruelly maimed the bodies of so many, is still the theme of sorrowful comment and wonder. A community, which has accepted earthquake, fire, flood and vigilance committees with stoical fortitude, seems almost paralyzed with this shock. To understand this thoroughly, the details of the explosion, its locality and unexpectedness must be taken into account.

Wells, Fargo & Co.'s establishment is perhaps one of the most vital business centers of San Francisco. Situated at the confluence of two tides—at a point where a great business thoroughfare and the principal avenue of fashion intersect—the corner of Montgomery and California streets, it overflows with animation and life. It is the focus of all interior news, gossip and dispatch; its letter department is crowded night and day; a back and fashionable club room are beneath its roof— in brief, it is a perfect microcosm. At noon on the 16th inst., its aspect was suddenly changed. In the hight of this animation and energy, when the sidewalks were crowded with promenaders and the club-room with people sitting down to their luncheons, a terrific concussion shook the ground within the circuit of a mile. From the rear of the building a column of dust and smoke shot upward to the hight of two hundred feet. The air was filled with flying splinters, bricks and mortar. In less than two minutes, the busy street was blocked and impassable; ropes were stretched around the building, and maimed and blackened bodies, but a few moments before full of life and energy, were borne away from its doors. The first intimation of the horrible disaster was conveyed to people two squares distant by portions of human limbs and fragments of burnt and blackened human flesh falling around them. Part of a skull was lodged in an opposite doorway, the lungs and viscera of some victim spattered the threshhold of one who came out to learn the cause of the explosion, and, on adjacent roofs, arms, legs, bones and ragged clothing fell in a shower.

The explosion, whose sound was sufficiently alarming—totally unlike the discharge of cannon, but having a profundity and volume that was peculiarly ominous—brought everybody to their feet. In an instant the streets in the vicinity were full of people, who narrowly escaped injury from the fragments of broken glass that were still falling from shattered windows. For a few minutes all was bewilderment. The locality of the explosion was the subject of a thousand rumors. One report located it in the Pine street mills, another in the assay office of G. W. Bell, in the rear of the express building, over which the smoke and dust still portentiously hung. It was not until some of the bodies had been recovered, and the ruins partly cleared away, that either the exact situation or the cause of the disaster was ascertained. The terrible power thus suddenly loosed was contained in a box of nitro-glycerine, which had been forwarded by the express company in ignorance of its contents, and which had exploded in the court-yard as a few unsuspicious employees of the company were opening it to discover the amount of loss by leakage. The blow of a hammer had broken the spell, which bound this destructive agent, and roused it to terrible activity.

An examination of the rear building, which was totally demolished, not alone gives an idea of the frightful energy employed by the expanding gases. Windows were shattered and doors broken in, four or five squares distant. Four of the victims were literally blown to atoms. Shreds and fragments that were never identified were picked up. It was estimated that over $60,000 worth of glass was destroyed within the circuit of half a mile. The tremendous concussion of the atmosphere was singularly exhibited in some cases. People dining in the club room over the court yard were thrown from their chairs to the ceiling. Those who were sitting received little injury; the waiters, who were standing or running about in attendance on the guests, were all seriously hurt. In one instance, the door of a room overlooking the rear building was blown in, and the occupant blown out of the same aperture, by the elastic rebound of the atmosphere. A passer-by was hurried by some unseen power diagonally across the street, and left in the doorway, without any other sensation than that of extreme bewilderment. Men who were near the point of explosion, but who escaped with but slight scratches from broken glass, felt at the time no serious annoyance from the concussion, but have since suffered from faintness and swelling of the limbs, proving that the system had unconsciously received a severe shock.

The accident was followed by much excitement and no little incoherency and ill-advised action. The proceedings of the board of supervisors was the farce that followed the tragedy. The chief of police was ordered to enter the dwellings and the houses of the citizens and destroy this objectionable chemical compound wherever found! It was resolved that a telegram should be sent to New York requesting shippers not to send any more nitro-glycerine to this market! In ordinary conversation a good many of those arguments which were formerly used against gunpowder, steam, electricity, chloroform and all startling inventions and discoveries, were promulgated with much heat and incoherency. I have heard it gravely asserted that it ought to be declared a criminal act to prepare the compound.

The steamer of the 18th carried a full list of the killed and wounded. The business community have met a severe loss in the death of Samuel

Knight, the superintendent of the express company. San Francisco has lost one of its most upright and faithful councilors in the person of G. W. Bell, the assayer, who is no less mourned in the private walks of society. The prominence and public reputation of Wells, Fargo & Co. had imparted to all its employees a certain prestige and popularity which give to their loss the aspect of a public calamity. During the afternoon following the incident, the office was besieged by crowds of solicitous friends; on the day of the funeral of the victims, business was partially suspended in the city.

The inquest has been held, and a verdict inculpating the shippers of the box has been found. From the evidence elicited it appears that a quantity of nitro-glycerine is now en route to this place. This fact, added to the terrible news just received of the destruction of the English steamer at Aspinwall, through this same fearful agency, has excited the liveliest alarm for the safety of the steamer now due. Otherwise the excitement has worn away, for this is a recuperative climate and a self-adjusting community. On steamer day, the express office was crowded, not by the curious and sympathizing of the day before, but by hard-faced businessmen with "speculation" in their eyes, and the energy of steamer day in their faces. The "dead have buried their dead"—the blood stains have been washed from floor and ceiling, workmen have cleared away the debris of the fallen walls, and the sound of hammering mingles with the hum of trade. The steamer took away a full list of freight—none the less full that the same busy fingers which had perhaps handled it were forever stilled, or that the papers containing the details of the terrible affair, went with other packages.

F.B.H.

LETTER 8

Christian Register, 21 July 1866

[From Our Regular Correspondent.]

CALIFORNIA.

San Francisco, May —, 1866.

Mr. Stephen Venard of Nevada has been lately made the recipient of a "handsomely-mounted Henry's rifle" from the hands of Wells, Fargo & Co. This is a generous community, and people are every day presented with tokens of admiration and esteem from their grateful fellow-citizens, but there is something in this peculiar gift worthy of passing comment. It was Mr. Venard's high privilege to forcibly remove from existence three robbers who had possessed themselves of Wells, Fargo & Co.'s treasure-boxes, by stopping the Nevada stage, in the fashion of Turpin, Duval and other noted highwaymen. The manner in which Mr. Venard executed his self-devoted mission commends itself to the California heart, and recalls the classic engagement of the Horatii and Curatii. On the arrival of the despoiled stage at Nevada, Mr. Venard, alone and armed only with a repeating rifle, sallied forth in the name of justice and inexorable law. Entering a *canon* he detected a head and revolver behind a rock. He hastily drew up his rifle, fired and brought down robber No. l. A few yards further he detected another head and revolver and a request "not to shoot." Calm and resistless as fate, the terrible Venard only drew a bead upon the head, and exterminated robber No. 2. At this, robber No. 3 started from his rock to run. The swift bullet of Venard's repeater brought him to his knees crippled. On hands and feet, he still endeavored to crawl away. Did the stoical Venard weakly hesitate? No! Crack went his repeater again, and the survivor of this luckless trio yielded up his miserable existence. Super-sensitive people and women might object to this deliberate killing of the last crippled felon, but I am satisfied that the artistic completeness of the catastrophe required his sacrifice, while the excellence of the shooting is sufficient to commend the act to every local Californian heart. In a civilized community, where property is more valuable than life, where horse-stealing is punishable by statute with death, (if the jury so decide) three men, more or less, are of little account. The trouble and annoyances of arrest, the expense of imprisonment, the uncertainty which frequently attends the trial by jury, and insufficiency of evidence to convict, were quietly stopped by the repeater of the gallant Venard.

A little pamphlet, which I have lately perused, published in this city, bears somewhat upon this subject. It is the "confession" of one Jenkins —"the murderer of eighteen men." This representative man came to an untimely end in this country two years ago, but not until he had given to a phonographic reporter a characteristic history of his life. In describing the killing of one of his victims, he tells us that he afterwards paced the distance from where he fired to where the man fell. I have forgotten the number of feet and inches, but am ready to agree with him that it was "a good shot." He attributes the commission of the fatal deed for which he was finally arrested and condemned to death to the effect of whiskey. "If it had not been for whiskey, I should not have killed O'Brien, and killed him in such a *careless* manner." Let our temperance friends record this fact. That thoughtlessness which may ruin even the most deliberately contrived destruction of a fellow being, may thus be traced directly to the "poisoned bowl." That "incivility and procrastination" which De Quincy fears may be produced by the habit of murder when too freely indulged, is of little moment, compared to the "carelessness" produced by the indulgence in intoxicating stimulants.

LETTER 9

Christian Register, 14 July 1866

[From our Regular Correspondent.]

CALIFORNIA.

San Francisco, June, 1866.

A cloud of dust, opaque and impervious, flies past my window. At the corner it precipitates three or four hats, a boy's cap, a tin sign, a chimney-pot, and other unconsidered trifles. The air is filled with driving sand, as palpable and stinging as the volley of arrows which the Lilliputians discharged at Gulliver. Pedestrians are scudding before the gale or facing it with that peculiar contraction of the eyebrow which becomes habitual to San Franciscans, and is certificate of their citizenship. Ladies in dreadfully disorganized drapery dive into doorways, or stop short, discomfitted and bewildered. It is hot in the sun and cold in the shade. The outlying fog already begins to slip past the encircling hills; before midnight it will invest the city, encamping on the marshes, or soothing like a cold poultice the wind-shaded surfaces and angles of the city. The green fields are rapidly disappearing before the advancing snow-drifts. The few stunted trees and shrubs in the gardens are beginning their half-yearly wrestle for existence with wind and drought. I know by these signs that the summer has come—the gentle season apostrophized by Thomson, but cursed by San Franciscans, is here. Verily, "the hounds of spring are on winter's traces" with a vengeance, baying and yelping somewhat more forcibly than Mr. Swinburne ever conceived.

But there are other influences besides the weather to remind you that you are in San Francisco. There comes a still, calm morning when you are sitting at your desk, feeling, perhaps, a little languid, for the air, though soft and warm, is oppressive, and seems in some odd way to have clogged and muffled your vitality. Your dog crosses the room restlessly, yawns, and changes position, and infects you with his nervousness. If a stranger, you will attribute these symptoms to the spring weather; if an old resident you will find yourself in the attitude of expectancy. Suddenly a slight thrill communicates itself to your desk. You turn to the dog, but he sits in another corner looking at you with startled and wishful eyes. If you have never felt this thrill before, you dismiss the phenomena at once from your mind; but if you have felt it, you rise quickly for you fear that the worst—how much worse you dare not think—is yet to come. A pause, and it comes. The door-bell peals an announcement of the invisible trespasser. There is no mistaking it now, be you stranger or resident. This is the tread which overthrew the Egyptian cities, which stamped a chasm for luckless Lisbon, and leveled Caraccas and Manilla. How the windows rattle and the strong beams over your head creak and disjoint. You make your way staggeringly to the door which opens and shuts in your face. As you are wondering how long this will continue the shaking suddenly ceases. The time has seemed interminable, and yet, if you have been cool enough to take out your watch you will find that ten seconds limits your experience. You flatter yourself you have been cool and collected until you find a piece of plaster like the icing of a plum-cake lying on your desk, and one or two fragments in your pocket, which you cannot account for.

Without entering into any theory of their terrestial disturbances, I think the fact of their having been preceded, accompanied, or followed, usually by some meteorological phenomena, is pretty well established. The morning of the great shock of the 8th October was ushered in with a smart shower of rain before sunrise, quite unusual for the season, as our rains seldom begin before November. The three or four shocks we have felt this spring have been attended with similar peculiarities of temperature and weather; when it is remembered that the evidences in regard to internal convulsions has not been clearly adduced—that the shocks are not experienced by people walking or standing on the earth's surface—there seems to be some reason in the theory of electrical superficial storms which has been lately promulgated. I was walking upon the beach on the northern shore of the city, during the shocks of October 8, 1865, and felt neither agitation of the earth nor saw any disturbance of the water, although within a few hundred yards windows were shattered, crockery thrown from shelves, and people shaken from their beds.

L E T T E R   1 0

Springfield Republican, 18 July 1866
Springfield Weekly Republican, 18 July 1866

FROM SAN FRANCISCO.

The Climate—The Watering Places—Commencement at the California
College—The New Registry Law—Edwin Forrest.

[From Our Special Correspondent.]

San Francisco, June 11, 1866.

Is the climate of California changing? is the question now generally
asked. The late unprecedented rains, the lowering and clouded skies,
the alternations of heat and cold so unlike our usual clear and equable
—though not exactly romantic—spring weather, seems to indicate a
radical change in the climate. Hitherto we have borne the afternoon
gales and foggy nights of our dry season with the calm consciousness that each succeeding morning would bring with it the clear sky,
bright sunshine and crisp, exhilarating atmosphere which have made
our summer mornings so notable. We seem to have borrowed the
uncertainty and capriciousness of your climate without parting with
the disagreeable features of our own. The wind, which usually blows
from an unclouded sky with the sober steadiness that belongs to six
months practice, has become gusty, flighty and fickle; the rain has lost
its dignified permanence and sincerity, and exhausts its strength in
hysterical showers and impotent squalls. Possibly, as the country is still
young, nature may not have settled into steady habits. Perhaps cholera,
rinderpest and the few smart earthquake shocks we have lately experienced may have had their influence. I doubt if cholera could obtain
a foothold here under the ordinary conditions of our climate. The
afternoon gales, which are strong enough to buffet the vitality out of
any poison or malaria, completely changes the air and temperature
of the city twice a day. Unless the broad Pacific, from whence these
sanitary zephyrs blow, be itself infected, we would stand in little dan-

ger of the epidemic. The sea is our sanitarium—the west wind our scavenger and health officer. Under its regime, vegetable and animal matter have no chance to decay, but are withered, dried up and blown away. Inhumation on this coast is a matter of civilization and luxury rather than of necessity. The defunct San Franciscan exposed on one of his native sand hills would be quietly and decently resolved into his original elements in a very short time.

Notwithstanding this unusual weather, our watering places are rapidly filling up. In the quality and variety of mineral springs we excel the Atlantic states. Combinations that exhaust the formulæ of chemistry, and temperatures ranging from zero to the boiling point, may be found at our different Spas. But we have no Newport, Nahant, or Cape May. A cold current washes the coast from Port Oxford to Monterey; the few bays which indent the shore line modify, but scarcely shelter you from the strong summer gales. Santa Cruz, with a good hotel and picturesque mountain and ocean views, is the closest approximation we can make to the seaside resorts of the East, but even this is too rude and ungenial. In the pastoral and cultivated aspects of nature we fail utterly. There are no farms—the word is unknown in the Californian vocabulary—nor meadows. Vast *ranches*, with fields of giant wild oats line the road-sides. The orchards, though prolific for their youth, seem dwarfed and stunted to eastern eyes, and are poor apologies for the wide-spread and arching boughs of northern homes. There are fine studies for the artist, grand details, and the heroics of nature, but the "bucolics" are wanting. The tourist would do well to dismiss from his mind any idea of shepherdesses, purling brooks, pastoral piping and lying on the grass. His shepherdess will turn out to be Mexican or halfbreed, his purling brook will be dry, his recumbent position on the field of wild oats will remind him of the martyred Christian on his bed of spikes, and will probably give him rheumatism. But if he has a good team, a comfortable carriage, and an eye for the picturesque, he can drive all day through rolling grain and wild mustard, exquisite in their gradations of color; or taking the mountain road, can wind through bosky *canadas* thick with variegated foliage, from the yellowish green of the willow to the dark olive of the evergreen, or ascending, look down deep gorges and *canons*, where, hundreds of feet below, the tops of tall pines show dimly, and the white foam of the mountain torrent flashes and is lost, or reaching the summit glance over spacious valleys opening into each other like a chain of lakes, to where other ranges sixty miles distant seem in the clear atmosphere to be outlined like black *silhouettes* against the cold leaden blue of a California sky. His experience will be interesting, various, and—expensive. For traveling in this country is a continual disbursement, and you calculate your distance, and the time you are absent from home not by miles and hours but by dollars and cents.

"Alma mater floreat." The college of California had its commencement on the 6th inst., after which the associated alumni of the Pacific coast held their second annual festival. Graduates of all the colleges, from stately Harvard and Yale to the more youthful academies and institutes of the West, were represented. A glance at the catalogue shows a formidable list of those entitled to academic honor. The oldest living graduate on the coast appears to be Andrew Williams of Union —class of 1819, from which, if I mistake not, W. H. Seward graduated; the youngest, of course, were those to whom the college of California had, but a few hours before, delivered her parchments. The festival, as may be imagined, was very enthusiastic. Gray-headed men recognized in their next neighbors old college chums and classmates from whom they had been separated for years. Hard-headed, close-fisted business men, who never seemed to have known any other education than that of money-getting, revived old college jokes, sang "Omni bene" and "Dulce, dulce domium" and misquoted classic school themes most villainously. Old pioneers, toughened by hard fortune and hard weather, talked of x and y, and attempted Latin verses. Whether these genial old boys carried their enthusiastic reminiscences to the point of sallying forth to wrench off knockers or forcibly remove the signs of the classic city of Oakland, I cannot say.

The speeches were capital. Perhaps I am not entirely free from our California egotism, but I doubt whether their average excellence could have been equaled in an eastern assembly of the same number. The oration before the associated alumni was delivered by Judge Shafter. It was a fair performance, but by no means equal to the address of Rev Horatio Stebbins, before the half-dozen graduates of the California college. This duty, which was assigned to Dr Scudder but declined by that gentleman as subordinate and inferior, was undertaken by Mr Stebbins at a late hour. Nevertheless I think no one was disappointed at the change. The address was a finished, logical and most forcible production, replete with truths that were remembered long after the brilliancies of the post-prandial alumni speeches were forgotten.

The new registry law—making the registration of all voters an indispensable preliminary to the exercise of suffrage—is in active operation. But a glance at the great register now open at the city hall shows an undue prevalence of such prefixes as "Mac" and "O" which have become identified with the democratic party, and so far but few well known republican names. There is great fear that the design of this law will be frustrated—that the next election may be lost by default, through the sheer neglect and indifference of Union citizens. It is a lamentable fact that except under such circumstances as a presidential election, or some local excitement, the republican votes cast in this city fall far short of the numerical strength of the party. Many respectable Union men do not go to the polls at all. When to this indifference is added the trouble of registry, it can easily be conceived that unless something be done to arouse the patriotism and energy of the republican party over one-half their vote will be lost. The democrats, meanwhile, are not idle—better politicians and with little else to do, they will make good use of that time which republican business men foolishly begrudge as taken from their labors.

Edwin Forrest is drawing crowded houses at Maguire's opera house, despite occasional severe criticism. Disclaiming any critical attitude myself, I think age has somewhat subdued the powerful predominance of the physical in his acting. His genius is more mellow. He agreeably surprised me in Richelieu, and in the quieter roles I think gives more general satisfaction. His popularity was at first imperilled by the mistaken zeal of his manager, who doubled the price of admission. The result convinced him of his error. The old prices were restored, and the house was at once crowded.   F.B.H.

LETTER 11

Christian Register, 28 July 1866

[From our Regular Correspondent.]

CALIFORNIA.

San Francisco, June 30, 1866.

The Sunday question has been lately revived in this city. A week or two ago, in the course of some remarks upon the proper observance of the Sabbath, the Rev. Dr. Stone, late of your city, held the press of San Francisco responsible for what he considered the desecration of that day by the people. The subject is in itself a delicate one, and the impression generally obtains that the Doctor, in a bold attempt to grapple it, has allowed its more subtle points to slip through his fingers, or has borrowed, in his zeal, the logic of the Donnybrook disputants and hit the first head he saw. The newspapers here, reflect rather than forecast public sentiment; they have generally ignored the subject; their offence, is at least a negative one, and the Doctor's remarks have only provoked raillery and opposition. It is unfortunate that he should have engaged as an adversary, that power which he could have easily used as an ally—one with which a majority of the people usually side in such issues, and which, in my opinion, is apt to take the broadest view of the subject.

THE SAN FRANCISCO SABBATH.

To look at the facts of the case seriously, they are by no means as dreadful as the Doctor's rhetoric would imply. That the San Francisco Sabbath is not the old Puritan conception of the "Lord's day" may be easily imagined. But that it is indecorous, dissipated, boisterous, or obtrusively irreverent, is not true. That portion of our population who make it a day of recreation, do so without interfering with or disturbing the devotions of their neighbors. The proportion of regular attendants upon divine service is greater than in any other commercial city of the Union, of equal population. When we take into consideration the peculiarities of our climate, which, while it renders weekly relaxation from toil absolutely necessary, is not conducive to thoughtful or contemplative rest, the foreign education and habits of a large class of society, the Catholic tastes of the early founders, and the cosmopolitan origin of the city, this proportion seems creditable. Dr. Stone has either made that superficial analysis and hasty generalization, pardonable in the new comer, or has "seriously inclined" his ear to the lugubrious tale of some dyspeptic deacon. But granting that San Franciscans are apt to make this sacred day one of enjoyment and recreation, that they are more inclined to follow instinct than duty, that the attendance at the orthodox churches is not what it should be, it will be difficult to make the public believe that the evil can be remedied by invoking the doubtful assistance of the public press. If Sabbath-breakers prefer the fellowship and social communion of picnics and junketings to the formal attitude of devotion, a little more humanity and kindness and a little less theology and austerity in the church might win them back. Sunshine and fresh air in the sermon might attract the rurally disposed. Californians do not take kindly to moral legislation on this subject; they do not return easily to the forms and regulations of older civilizations, and the missionary who attempts their conversion must throw aside creeds and forms, and exhort from the broad platform of humanity and love. The work of regeneration goes on slowly, and it would be unwise to hasten it. Every reflective man knows that within the past twelve years a wonderful change has taken place in the social and moral aspect of the city, and that the dancing-halls and German gardens which formerly occupied public thoroughfares have disappeared. But when the treasurer of the Christian Commission, less than a year ago, refused to accept a contribution because it was the pecuniary result of a private theatrical entertainment, public sentiment was shocked. People who had accepted Sunday theatricals for many years could not appreciate the subtle moral turpitude involved in private theatricals whose proceeds were intended for patriotic, benevolent and Christian purposes.

THE SANCTITY OF WEDNESDAY EVENING.

But Dr. Stone's later enunciation of the peculiar sanctity of Wednesday evening—the prayer-meeting night of the Orthodox churches—

was perhaps the logical sequitur to his Sabbatarian arguments. It appears that the Deaf and Dumb Asylum—one of the noblest charities in the State—has an annual examination in June, and its managers thoughtlessly selected a Wednesday evening for that purpose. The announcement was read on the previous Sunday in all the churches. Dr. Stone, however, profited by the occasion, to pointedly rebuke this manifest desecration of the evening, and after assuring his congregation that he would not attend, trusted that they would also be found in their accustomed places. The *Pacific*, a religious weekly, (Orthodox) commented also upon this oversight of the managers, and wondered at the Doctor's "condescension in reading the notice at all!" In both instances the Christian and benevolent purposes of the meeting were admitted. In spite of this infelicitous introduction, the attendance at the examination was very large, enthusiastic and sympathizing. A collection was taken up and a handsome sum subscribed by many church-members who, perhaps, preferred this active participation in benevolence and good works, to even prayer and supplication. The Rev. Horatio Stebbins, with a forcible and pathetic appeal, prefaced the exercises. They were instructive and interesting, showing great proficiency in the pupils and thoughtful care of instructors, and were, in a literary sense, perhaps not inferior to the regular Wednesday evening petitioning. Every one appeared pleased and satisfied; the poor little objects of charity looked happy and radiant, notwithstanding that—to quote the just language of the *Pacific*—"in twenty-seven churches, at that moment, prayers were being offered to the Most High." Let us trust that in their orisons, the sins of these misguided, but well-meaning men, who took that occasion to sympathize with the least of God's creatures, were duly remembered.

THE EPISCOPAL BISHOP AND CHURCH
ON SLAVERY AND LOYALTY.

The *Pacific*, mentioned above, should not be confounded with the *Pacific Churchman*, an Episcopal paper lately established in this city. I am tempted to quote a characteristic passage from the pastoral charge of the Bishop of California, published in the first number. Speaking of the attitude of the church, during the rebellion, he says: " The only 'slavery' recognized by them was the bondage of man to the sinful world; the only loyalty they professed, was that of the church to

Christ." This statement in its negative quality is strictly true of the church on this coast. During the four years of the nation's terrible struggle for existence, the Episcopal church by word or deed never signified any sympathy with the principle for which the North was contending; no flag ever waved from its spires; no God-speed to the work; no supplication for the success of our arms were ever uttered from its pulpits. The formal prayer of the bishop was simply a confession of blood-guiltiness and a supplication for peace-at-any-price. In the service the war-like utterances of the prophets were carefully avoided, and in one instance—a national fast day—when the appropriate hymn was given out, two verses which supplicated the overthrow of our enemies were pointedly omitted. A few wealthy and bitter secessionists in the church, acting upon the fears of a weak-minded and timid clergy, completely controlled all ecclesiastical expression. Looking at the quotation I have taken from the bishop's letter in the light of these facts, it reads very much like a wretched subterfuge—a despicable apology for moral cowardice and temporal subserviency before which the outspoken disloyalty of Dr. Scott (driven from his church by an indignant mob, for praying for a Southern President) is pardonable in the sight of God, and manly and respectable in the opinion of humanity. In speaking of the Episcopal church I use the term in its abstract and general sense. There were one or two individual exceptions, and that of the Rev. Mr. Hill, of Sacramento, who was a bold and out-spoken friend of the Union under quite as difficult conditions, is deserving of especial commendation.

Beyond a text for the above remarks, I do not know that the *Pacific Churchman* furnishes anything of interest. A new pastor for the new church of St. James—chiefly remarkable for its boy choir—is daily expected. Among his eligibilities for the priestly office should be remembered a particularly artistic capacity for "intoning."

The Rev. Mr. Ames, has not, I believe, accepted the call from Santa Cruz. I should not wonder if he were beguiled into it by the attractions, a fine climate and rare scenery, for it is the Newport of the State, and during the summer season his audiences would be as metropolitan as he could find in San Francisco. The Rev. Horatio Stebbins has fairly recovered his pristine strength and vigor, but his active duties and untiring energy do not allow him to accumulate a reserved vitality.   H.

LETTER 12

Springfield Republican, 4 August 1866
Springfield Weekly Republican, 11 August 1866

FROM CALIFORNIA.

Summer on the Pacific Coast—The Fourth and the Negro—The Monadnock
and the Vanderbilt—Retributive Justice—San Francisco Moving to
Aid Portland.

[From Our Special Correspondent.]

San Francisco, July 9, 1866.

Midsummer! To Eastern readers, what a suggestion of green fields
and white-sleeved haymakers, of leafy screens and quiet pools with
lazy cattle standing mid-leg deep, of hazy mountain tops and shimmer-
ing landscapes! To dwellers in Atlantic cities, what visions of heated
pavements, of staring bricks, of grateful shade trees, of straw hats and
white muslin, are conjured up in this word. Alas, *here* it only suggests
that spring has vanished from field and meadow, and her colors are
replaced by the "sere and yellow"; that the soil on the great plains
begins to crack and yawn with drouth, that the rivers have dried up,
that the red dust flies on the mountain road, and that the wind blows
chilly from the northwest. In San Francisco it means equal proportions of fog and wind. On the evening of the Fourth of July it was a
pleasant and instructive sight to observe the population, in great-coats
and thick shawls, warming themselves by bonfires, watching the sky-
rockets lose themselves in the thick fog, and returning soberly home
to their firesides and warm blankets.

The Fourth was observed throughout the state with unusual enthusiasm and display. The civic celebration here was very fine, but its
moral effect was greatly marred by the weakness and want of nerve
of the committee and grand marshal. On the previous anniversary,
some trouble had arisen by the attempts of copperheads to keep the
negro out of the procession, and several Irish societies refused to join

if the negroes were allowed a place. Nevertheless, the colored people were admitted finally, and an attempt to insult them during the procession by a few rowdies, was promptly checked and resulted only in giving the negro a complete ovation during the rest of the march. This year the committee were weak enough to listen to the demand of citizens of doubtful loyalty to exclude a race whose loyalty had never been doubted, and poor Sambo was not invited. Their humble request to be allowed some place in the procession was refused, and, in the committee's anxiety to spare the sensitive prejudices of our Irish and southern fellow-citizens, an invitation extended to the Masonic body was rescinded so far as it referred to colored lodges. Such action would have been pitiable enough, had it expressed the weak prejudices of a majority, but being confined to a minority whose antecedents have not entitled their prejudices to much consideration from loyal citizens, the occurrence has excited considerable indignation. It is asserted that the committee chose between the Fenian brotherhood and the colored people, and accepted the terms they dictated—the exclusion of the negro. Their conduct is the more presumptuous from the fact that Californians are naturally cosmopolitan and liberal. In the earlier days the Chinese took part in our celebrations; only within the last few years have they been interdicted. The expression of the committee was totally unauthorized and gratuitous, and it is very improbable if the like will ever be attempted again to the disgrace of the city. The orator of the day, Dr Stone, very pointedly declared against any exclusiveness or prohibition, as inconsistent with the spirit of our institutions and the day. The ministerial union passed resolutions declaring the conduct of the committee as unchristian, and most of the pulpits promptly repudiated any sympathy with the sentiment that excluded the negro or Chinese.

I have but little news to chronicle. In an adventurous and energetic community, educated to hardship, tumult and excitement, it is not easy to say what events are sufficiently important to come under this classification. The reporter who can confidently count upon an earthquake or nitro-glycerine explosion takes but little pains to celebrate events of lesser magnitude. Hence the more subtle and delicate accomplishments of the profession are not cultivated here, the newspapers are often dull and gossips languish. There have been two or three mysterious murders here within the past few years worthy to have been chronicled by the hand that delineated the Williams and

Marr tragedies. It would have grieved De Quincey to have witnessed the mangling of these stories—a butchery quite as reckless as the one recorded.

The arrival of the Monadnock and her consort, the Vanderbilt created something akin to a sensation. The former vessel, which presented from the wharf only a view of two queer-looking towers, and a smoke stack apparently resting on the surface of the water, attracted the most attention. Not from her peculiar shape—for the Camanche, launched here a year or two ago, had familiarized us to this novel style of naval architecture—but from the fact that she had weathered, in this strange fashion, that stormy cape which most Californians hold in vivid recollection. The Monadnock has gone to Mare Island—the naval depot of the coast—where the Camanche, whose early history was a record of misfortune and expense, now lies in inglorious and forgotten obscurity. Whether we shall or shall not have occasion for the services of these vessels, it is certain that the status of republican power and importance on this coast is higher for their presence; the American citizen holds his head more erect, and it is easy to detect a decided strut in each "sovereign's" walk. With this feeling it may be imagined that the course of Commodore Rodgers at Valparaiso is not looked upon with favor. There is a cloudy and not clearly defined impression that the commodore ought to have blown the Spanish fleet out of water, for the sole reason, I fear, that he could easily have done so. While there has been no very active sympathy here for the defenseless condition of the Chilian government, there has been considerable satisfaction in the offensive capacity of our own, and the opportunity which Rodgers lost for assuming a belligerent and heroic attitude in the eyes of the English admiral, is bewailed with amusing sincerity.

The grand jury have indicted the Duane brothers for the murder of Col Ross, which occurred a month ago in one of our principal thoroughfares. The fatal shot was fired by the notorious Charles Duane. Although the character of his victim was none of the highest, the popular dislike of Duane, whose reputation for lawlessness and brutal aggression has long been established in California, may make this last act the culminating one of his career. If so, it will offer another instance of the slow but sure retributive justice which has overtaken those few desperate men whose deeds have stained the initial pages of California history with blood, and whose crimes asked the harsh but swift legislation of vigilance committee and lynch law. Duane, you may remember, was one of the gang expatriated by the last vigilance committee. Returning here, he commenced suit against the P.M.S.S.Co. for damages resulting from his illegal deportation, but without pecuniary success. Naturally a splendid animal, of powerful frame and fine physique, dissipation and disease at last reduced him to a paralytic cripple. He walked the streets with a crutch—the miserable wreck and shadow of his former self. He eked a subsistence from the remains of his ill-gotten property—a dispute about the title of which was the origin of his last affray. Whatever his fate, it would seem that life to this man, whose force lay only in his physical pre-eminence and whose enjoyments were solely sensual, could be of little satisfaction in his present helpless and impotent condition. But he has pursued the logic of his disastrous career, even as his brother exiles pursued theirs, to its bitter demonstration. Cora and Casey were hanged. Sullivan committed suicide. Chris Lilly, who killed McCoy before entering upon his California career, returned to New York and his inevitable destiny—a death by violence. Mulligan, delirious from dissipation, killed the friends who were trying to restrain him, and was at last brought to bay, and shot down like a wild beast. The sole survivor of this wretched confederacy lies to-day in a felon's cell, awaiting his fate. The same system of compensation might be traced through some more respectable examples. Many of our chivalrous southern and southwestern knights errant, who have had their hands washed of blood by legal quibbles, political judges and barbaric jurymen, have at last met retribution from the bowie-knife or pistol of some other self-elected avenger. Smith, who butchered Newell in cold blood, and was acquitted because the jury found justification in some slanders which the victim had repeated about Smith's wife, was recently shot in Virginia City. Showalter, and many of the professional duellists, have also gone the way of their victims.

Forrest is seeking recreation and physical invigoration at the springs. As the mail closes some steps are being taken toward the relief of the Portland sufferers whose call for aid has just reached us. The telegraph will have informed you of the result before this reaches you.

F.B.H.

LETTER 13

Christian Register, 11 August 1866

[From Our Regular Correspondent.]

CALIFORNIA.

San Francisco, July 14, 1866.

The "Fourth," with its parade, oration, bonfires, fireworks, and exhilarating bustle and confusion, is over. Unhappily there lingers a disagreeable recollection of the conduct of the executive committee, who excluded the negro from participation in the celebration. The fact was discovered too late for opposition without disorganizing the entire arrangements. In thus yielding to the prejudices of a few disloyal and ignorant people, the committee have disgraced the city, and now that the passions of partisans are cooled, and the fears of politic men soothed, people are generally ashamed, and there is a disposition even among the most rabid negro-haters to shift the responsibility upon the committee.

The act was wholly gratuitous. As a community, Californians are innately liberal. That very materialism which is a peculiar and often objectionable feature of our civilization, keeps us from yielding to cant, prejudice or conservatism of any kind, however justified by precedent or authority. The tone of Californian society,—hard, satirical, incisive, iconoclastic and disillusive,—is inimical to humbug in any shape. Some of the Orthodox clergy denounced the action of the committee as unchristian and unpatriotic. The ministerial convention, (Congregational) passed resolutions condemnatory of it. Dr. Stone, orator of the day, characterized it as inconsistent with the sentiment honored in the celebration. Had this thing occurred on the anniversary a year previous, the rebuke might have been still more pointed—the Unitarian clergyman to whom the responsible office of orator was then delegated, in all probability would have refused to act for a committee that represented neither nationality nor equality.

The excluded race bore their humiliation with dignity and silence.

Only one circumstance was significant of their feeling. The Zion (colored) church, formerly the First Unitarian—where Thomas Starr King preached his first sermon, and in which the greater part of his pulpit ministry was spent—on that day showed no flag. The first church to raise the Stars and Stripes at the beginning of the war, never before on anniversary of victory or fast had its flagstaff lacked the national emblem. Whether these people who felt for King a loyalty and devotion almost superstitious in its extent and fervor, really thought, that in their humiliation, some insult was offered to his memory, I cannot say. I know that they sincerely believe that with him died liberality and justice, and that had he lived they would have been spared this latest wrong.

The peculiar fascination which King's liberal and broad humanity exercised equally over all classes, even to the poorest and humblest, was something remarkable. Sometimes its effect was shown in characteristic and amusing, but always sincere and earnest, compliment. Mr. King was fond of repeating a conversation he once overheard while leaving church after a sermon in which he had occasion to refute several arguments in detail. "Convincing, wasn't it?" ejaculated the first critic. "Convincing! *He took every trick!*" was the reply.

Meetings for the aid of the Portland sufferers have been held here, called by the mayor; and Rev. Horatio Stebbins has undertaken to plead the cause of his former constituents. But in spite of his eloquence and fervor, it is very evident to the observer that the movement has excited but little enthusiasm and sympathy. It is no reflection on Mr. Stebbins's efforts, for San Francisco has done nothing for the destitute of Virginia City, lately devastated by fire, or Dayton, recently burned down,—both places much nearer home. In fact, San Francisco has little to spare for ostentatious charities, which, I fear, has been to a great extent the character of her benevolence. The Sanitary Commission was a magnificent expression of emulation and rivalry. King tickled the egotism of California with a compliment, and it chuckled to the tune of millions. Besides, it was in part payment for the immunity enjoyed by the State from the costly sacrifices of the civil war. It was King's humanity and King's poetry which elevated and consecrated the offering. Yet, with this show of liberality, it is a melancholy fact that the poor and destitute of San Francisco are comparatively in a worse condition than those of Eastern cities. The forms of suffering here, if of not so low an order, are quite as keen and poignant. While few would refuse a starving man a meal's victuals, there are many here who go hungry, and some who starve, rather than beg. Helpless and unfortunate men, the luckless and shiftless outcasts of an older civilization, exhaust their means and energies in getting to this imaginary Utopia—a country which, more than any other, exacts the greatest labor, endurance, energy and pluck, as the conditions of success. The prizes offered are often high, but the blanks are many and frequent. Most of the avenues of employment are thronged. A majority of the immigrants are, of course, only fitted for clerks or accountants, of which there are already too many. In the professions, which are also overstocked, mediocrity has no chance. Consider, also, the fluctuations in business, here conducted often in the most reckless manner; stock gambling; inundations, fires and robberies, more frequent here than in Eastern cities; the extravagance of living; and you will find more superinducing causes for poverty and reverses than elsewhere. The only popular relief for these troubles has been a peculiarly Californian one—suicide. Insanity has helped others into oblivion. But, save one society, lately incorporated, there has been no organized system of benevolence. The city which gave so munificently to the Sanitary Commission has been without an almshouse.

Prof. Bolander, of the State geological survey, in a recent paper to the Californian Academy of Natural Sciences, has sounded the alarm against the reckless destruction of the few forest trees which belong to the Coast Ranges near this treeless peninsula. The redwood spoken of is a peculiarly Californian institution:—

Another great beneficial feature in this species is the power it possesses in condensing fogs and mists. A heavy fog is always turned into a rain, wetting the soil and supplying springs with water during the dry season. Springs in and near the redwoods are never in want of a good supply of water, and crops on the Coast Ranges are not liable to fail. The year of 1864 has proved my assertion beyond doubt; this fact is generally known—a great deal of land has been taken up since. It is my firm conviction that if the redwoods are destroyed—and they necessarily will be if not protected by a wise action of our government—California will become a desert, in the true sense of the word. On their safety depends the future welfare of the State; they are our safeguard. It remains to be seen whether we shall be benefited or not by the horrible experience such countries as Asia Minor, Greece,

Spain and France have made by having barbarously destroyed their woods and forests. But with us here it is even of a more serious nature; wise governments would be able to replace them in those countries; but no power on earth can restore the woods of California when once completely destroyed!

Perhaps for this reason the fogs in this treeless city merely fulfil their mission by enwrapping us in an uncomfortable and chilly blanket. As I write, the prospect from my window is fast being obliterated. It is midsummer by the almanac, but the "sea-coal fire" by which I sit is much more consistent with the facts. In winter fires are merely a luxury,—lightening the gloom of a cloudy, rainy day, or taking the office of candles in the brief twilight; in summer they are a necessity.   H.

LETTER 14

Christian Register, 25 August 1866

[From our Regular Correspondent.]

CALIFORNIA.

San Francisco, July 28, 1866.

In this dreary summer season, made up of bewildering winds and fogs, so depressing as to be almost suicidal in their tendencies, it is some relief to stroll through the markets and satisfy oneself that the climate produces something better than such meteorological phenomena. For in no other country are the fruits as picturesque and showy. Golden pumpkins that might have contained Cinderella's coach without great stretch of the imagination; potatoes, like small boulders, but clear-skinned and pink-eyed; cabbages, graceful in outline—perfect Brobdignagian roses; radishes, "pink as Aurora's finger tips," but somewhat large for that goddess; beets of a preposterous bigness and carrots of exasperating length, heap the stalls of the green-grocer. Further on are strawberries—(the larger ones are out of season, but

five of these immature specimens fill a saucer); blackberries, raspber-
ries and currants equally large, cherries that you might make "two
bites" at without fastidiousness; peaches, plums, apricots and their
twin brothers, the nectarines, apples and pears, all together, until the
eye is wearied with their variety and succession. Grapes are coming
in; a month later they will take possession of the market to the exclusion of other fruits. Nothing is so wonderful to the stranger as the
extraordinary quality, quantity and variety of the grapes in California.
It is almost the only fruit which in flavor and delicacy really surpasses
Eastern products. For, in spite of size and prolific bearing, with this
exception, the pomological exhibition of this country is deceitful; your
mammoth strawberries are stringy, your pears are fibrous, your large
apples are Dead Sea fruit, and your magnificent looking peaches are
leathery. But the grape alone is sincere. The native variety is almost
indescribable—an epicurean combination of the cherry and the grape
with a certain flavor that escapes analysis. All the foreign vines flourish
splendidly here; the Muscat with its perfumed sweetness, the luscious
Malaga, and several varieties from the south of Europe ripen on our
hillsides, with all the condensed sunshine of Italian skies under their
glossy skies.

With this remarkable excellence in the quality and productiveness
of the grape, it is not singular that vine-growing is beginning to rival
even the mining interests and divide the attention of capitalists. As
yet, the manufacture of wine is crude, and our manufacturers lack
experience. California has no wine cellars; the wine-grower,—in that
disposition to realize quickly, which is one of the worst features of
California speculation,—sends his wines to market, fresh from the
press. Yet the average quality of the product of our vintages have attracted the attention of foreign merchants. Sir Morton Peto says of its
extent:—

> "The wine product of California alone would be a source
> of wealth to any country. In 1855 California did not number
> 1,000,000 vines; in 1862 she had under cultivation upwards of
> 10,500,000, and in 1863 she produced 350,000 gallons of wine
> and brandy, which was estimated in 1865 to have increased to
> 1,000,000."

The moral aspect of this new feature of our resources is beginning to
exercise the fears of our temperance brethren. Rev. E. J. Lacey, former

pastor of the First Congregational Church in San Francisco, now on a tour in Europe, writes to the *Pacific* as follows:—

> I wish now to tell you what I have observed in wine-growing countries, and to give you the result of many inquiries concerning the drinking habits of the people. The testimony of travelers in Europe, as far as I ever heard, was to the effect that intoxication was very little known in wine-producing districts, and that if wines were only cheap and unadulterated in America the vices of intemperance would be greatly abated, if not entirely removed. I was so well convinced by such unanimous testimony that I regarded the introduction of the wine culture in California, and its general increase, as a harbinger of general morality.
>
> I have just spent six months in a country place of Switzerland, where the people do nothing but work in their vineyards; where wine is cheap and pure, and far more the beverage of the laboring classes than water; where none think of making a dinner without a bottle of wine; where all the scenery about is of the most elevating and ennobling character. Here more intoxication was obvious than in any other place it was ever my lot to live in. The common people passing to and fro with loads of hay or wood, or to and from their markets, would become intoxicated before reaching home, the wine shops or cafés along the roads at all hours were frequented, and at almost any time of the day might be found full of men.
>
> On holidays and festal occasions you might suppose all the male population drunk, so great are the numbers in this deranged and beastly condition. On Sunday afternoon young men go shouting along the street. Intelligent Germans informed me that this is the great social evil of their country, a place where wine, if not very cheap, is never adulterated, and where great quantities of it are drunk.

I am afraid that even though the doctor's individual experience is considered sufficient to overbalance the general testimony of travelers, the mere consideration of intemperance will not greatly influence the wine-growing interests of this coast. The *mines* have, I fear, been as productive of immorality as ever the *wines* promise to be, and yet the general progress of this country has been in the line of reform, enlightenment and Christianity. Few thoughtful men will believe that easy and familiar relations with the grape will lead to habits any worse than those superinduced by the intoxication of gold getting and its attendant excitements. The drunkenness which now obtains here, and is really slight in comparison with older civilizations, results from the use of vile alcoholic stimulants much more disastrous in their effects mentally and physically than the regular consumption of native wine. Anything that might be substituted for the doctored brandies, whiskies and bitters now in use, would be ultimately beneficial to the country.

The weather has been remarkably unpleasant even for the season. Thick fogs encompass the city and peninsula, night and day. Yet, twenty miles further south, you find cloudless skies and the transparent, dry atmosphere of a California summer. The disposition of these fog belts are often peculiar. Frequently when the city is enveloped in fog, a ride to the Cliff-House, four miles west, and apparently in the line of march of the incoming fog, brings you to the ocean sands glittering in the sunlight, and an open sea beyond, brightly flashing to the horizon line, without even the shadow of a cloud. This peculiarity, to a stranger unknown, gives a singular effect to the spectacle of open carriages, barouches and buggies, which may be seen on foggy, dismal mornings, slowly wending their way to the ocean beach and a more genial climate.

The Pacific branch of the Liberal Christian Church are pushing their work thoroughly. Since their organization, answers to their circulars have been received from all parts of the coast. Over seventy names are already enrolled; thirty or forty in Sacramento alone. The Rev. Mr. Ames has already visited this latter city and Stockton, with the purpose of effecting some parochial organization if possible. *Monthly Journals* have been distributed at different points, and the committee intend to send East for Unitarian tracts. I think that some specimen copies of the *Register* sent to the Branch for circulation, would be of benefit both to the *Register* and the organization here.   H.

LETTER 15

Springfield Republican, 29 August 1866
Springfield Weekly Republican, 1 September 1866

FROM CALIFORNIA.

Important Geological Discovery—California the Cradle of the Race—
Buried Treasures in San Francisco—Changes and Improvements in the
Pacific Metropolis—Need of a large Public Park—A Striking Instance of
Husbandly Affection—The Perils of the Miner's Life.

[From Our Special Correspondent.]

San Francisco, August 5, 1866.

California has claimed, among her remarkable productions, the most stupendous valleys, the largest trees, the biggest vegetables. She now appears before the world in the more ambitious character of being the oldest portion of the earth's surface, and, to use the remarkably fine language of the interior press, "the original cradle of the human race." The discovery of a human skull in the pliocene formation is the foundation of this startling assumption.

It appears that an honest miner, named James Matson, digging in a shaft in Calaveras county, came across this osseous fragment at the depth of two hundred and fifty feet. The relic passed into the hand of Scribner, merchant, who transferred it to Jones, doctor, who, in turn, handed it over to the state geological survey, where it exactly fitted a theory promulgated by the survey of the extreme antiquity of man on this coast. Professor Whitney has visited the shaft, and is confident that the position of the skull justifies him in ascribing its introduction to a period anterior to the lava deposits. This would make it antedate the mastodon, the pachyderms, and, indeed, most of the paleotheres. In fact, according to this latest theory, that which has been termed the pliocene formation is a comparatively recent deposit; the world is really older by many million years than hitherto supposed by geologists—particularly that portion known as the Pacific slope, to which the Laurentian hills of Agassiz are creations of yesterday. Under what conditions of atmosphere or climate our pliocene friend flourished is not known. From an unscientific view-point, which is the only one your correspondent would venture to take, the state of things must have been singularly unpleasant for this earliest pioneer. With the whole range of the Sierras a series of active volcanoes, with earthquakes by day, and eruptions by night, he must have passed a remarkably active existence in dodging the scoria and volcanic stones—those unrefreshing showers of the period. Huge Saurians contended with him for the limited refection of mussels and shell-fish. Defenseless,—for it is singular that no weapons—bows, arrows or spears—have been found among the rude domestic implements which denote his presence, and place him in the "stone age,"—he must have been an easy prey to the lower order of his animal contemporaries. The skull, which is not perfect, has a facial angle not unlike a Digger Indian. The bones are somewhat thicker than modern specimens—doubtless a providential precaution to enable it better to resist the local showers previously alluded to. The discovery has occasioned considerable excitement in scientific circles, and some little stir among theologians. Dr Jones is reported to have given concrete expression to the opinions of the latter, by remarking in a peculiarly Californian manner, as he took up the skull: "This knocks h-ll out of Moses!" The pliocene skull has been the text of some remarkable editorials in the up-country papers. The provincial editors have gambolled wildly in these geological "pastures new," and some theories have been advanced that would startle Agassiz, Lyell and Austed. Doubtless the Society of Pioneers will claim the skull as a member.

To turn to a more recent discovery, the workmen who are laying the foundation of the new Merchants' Exchange on California street, the other day unearthed a huge iron coffer, strongly secured by bolts and locks. A crowd rapidly collected, and various conjectures were made as to its probable contents. The site was formerly occupied by a wealthy firm who had been burnt out in one of the disastrous conflagrations of early days. Why might it not contain some forgotten treasure? The supposition was one that appealed to every California instinct; the lucky finders might have sold the sealed box on speculation at a very high figure. Its locks were finally broken, and its contents proved to be simply a few valueless books and papers. Although the result in this instance was unsatisfactory, there seems to be some foundation for the prevalent belief that is felt in these and similar treasure stories. But little is really known of the old pioneers. The conflagrations that sometimes spared a man's strong box burnt up both him and his record—nobody being the wiser, though it is whispered some were the wealthier. A singular extravagance and reckless disregard of things for the time valueless pervaded society. I remember, several years ago, to have been shown the foundations of a house near one of the wharves built up on boxes of plug tobacco, which, at the time it was laid, was worth less than the necessary, though scarcer, timber. It had been of course ruined by salt water. A sidewalk of the same material is said to have been once put down in front of what is now known as Montgomery block, on the principal avenue of the city.

The new Merchants' Exchange is to be a costly and extensive structure. This, with the new Mercantile Library building and Mechanics' Institute will give an added architectural beauty to a city which formerly lavished a greater part of its artistic taste on engine-houses and hotels. A Venetian style, with hanging windows and balconies, the ornamentation beginning at the second stories, leaving a "water base" below, is very common. The city is steadily pushing its way westward past the shifting sand-hills. The streets are stretching oceanward in long parallels. Those thoroughfares running north and south are being steadily widened and rebuilt to suit the exigencies of trade and travel. Kearney street will in a year rival our great boulevard—Montgomery street. Houses perambulate the principal avenues, and it is not unusual to find the perspective of some of the most familiar thoroughfares abruptly closed by one of these moving tenements. The visitor of three years ago would to-day hardly recognize the metropolis.

With these changes and improvements the necessity of providing for a large public park becomes daily more obvious. Olmsted's plan, submitted to the city, was large, liberal, comprehensive and practical, but I fear too liberal, too large, too comprehensive for this material—and, in such matters, narrow-minded—municipality. The idea of using so much ground and spending so much money for a mere promenade could not be entertained without suspicion and disfavor. Other plans, having more immediate reference to somebody's land, railroad, turnpike or homestead lots—in fact, having some direct pecuniary and speculative relation—were substituted. One supervisor was honest enough to say that he didn't see any necessity for a park at all; "that we had got along very well, so far, without one;" but the argument is too familiar to repeat.

An incident, so grotesquely horrible in its details that the pen of Hawthorne might have woven it into a romance, occurred a few days ago in this city. Complaint was made to the health officer that the occupant of a handsome residence in one of our fashionable quarters was creating a nuisance by keeping the corpse of his wife in the building, to the great discomfort and ill health of the neighborhood. It appears that the wife of the person complained of died about a year ago, when the husband purchased a metallic coffin and placed the corpse in one of the rooms of his residence. It was alleged more particularly that the day previous to the complaint he had taken the body from its coffin and washed it with a garden hose, afterward replacing it in the coffin where, at the time of the complaint, it still remained. Sincere as was this evidence of undying and unalterable affection, the spectacle of that stricken and inconsolable widower playing the garden hose upon the decomposed remains of his former partner seems to have been too much for the neighbors. The health officer thought so too, and the nuisance was abated. The whole picture, with its terrible mingling of the ghastly and ludicrous, requires no comment.

The casualties which are incident to mining are so frequent that the eye scarcely rests upon their record in the daily press, unless the accident is fatal or involves the life and limb of more than one fellow creature. I met the following paragraph in one of the Nevada papers. Eastern folks, who are enamored with the idea of a miner's life, should remember that the injury spoken of was incidental to labors that are compensated at the rate of two dollars per day and board:—

"The 'local' of the Reese River Reveille has been paying a visit to the county hospital, where, among other scenes of suffering, he observed a miner suffering from a compound fracture of the leg—the hospital being full of similar cases. A fortnight ago, emaciated and shriveled and shrunken to the merest anatomy, attacked by lockjaw, and almost lifeless, he was admitted into the county hospital, accompanied by the horrid mechanical appliances which had been devised to restore shape to the fractured limb. There were heavy semi-circular iron bands punched with holes in which threads had been cut for the reception of screws. The bands were applied to the leg, and screws were inserted into the holes and pressed against the ends of the protruding bones, to force them into place. The torture was dreadful and continued for weeks, but the bones still projected as they did at the moment of the accident. The wretched man lies there, his cheek suffused with the hectic flush, and symptoms of delirium in his eyes—lies there, waiting and hoping for strength to submit to the amputation of the most frightful looking limb that ever human eyes beheld."

F.B.H.

LETTER 16

Springfield Republican, 12 September 1866
Springfield Weekly Republican, 14 September 1866

FROM CALIFORNIA.

The Summer Street Accident—Thirty Persons Killed and Wounded—
Heroic Conduct of the Sufferers—Criminal Neglect of Property Owners
and Builders.

[From Our Special Correspondent.]

San Francisco, August 8, 1866.

Another terrible accident has just occurred, not a hundred yards from the scene of the nitro-glycerine explosion of April last. At 3 o'clock this morning the Summer Street House—a second class lodging tenement in a narrow street near Montgomery—fell to the ground, burying most of its occupants, about 25 in number, in the ruins. Happening at an hour when the city was wrapped in sleep, when the streets were deserted, and the darkness rendered rescue and relief difficult and dangerous, the catastrophe was in many respects even more appalling than the calamity at Wells, Fargo & Co.'s. For some minutes after the crash, the few people who happened to be in the vicinity were prevented by the cloud of dust and darkness from learning the extent of the disaster, or doing anything to assist the wounded, whose cries and groans filled the air. Providentially, some firemen, returning from a fire in the vicinity, gave the alarm, which brought out the entire force of the department. Bonfires were lit in the street, and when the dust cleared away, the building—of brick and three stories high—was found a mass of ruins, with only the front wall standing, that even then tottered to its fall. Undeterred by this danger, the courageous firemen at once stripped themselves to their arduous work, clearing away beams and rafters above the buried sufferers; but while in the act of releasing one helpless wretch the wall fell, crushing the unfortunate man and several of his brave deliverers. The crowd fell back with horror, and for a moment, fear seemed to paralyze them, but they speedily closed up and the task was recommenced with undiminished energy. As about 40 men were at work in the ruins when the wall fell, their escape seemed miraculous; fortunately, the wall, instead of tippling over en masse, seemed to crumble to dust, injuring only those immediately against it. Counting these, over thirty, more or less injured, were taken from the ruins. Of this number, nine were killed outright, three or four have since died of their injuries, and about sixteen or seventeen are wounded.

The following is a list of the killed as far as heard from: John Brewster, Jr., proprietor of the house, George Burbank, Charles W. Lawson, ——— McCready, painter, Peter Halley, Thomas Tweintyman, Leon Heal, Willie McCready, a boy, and three unrecognized bodies. These were exhibited at the deadhouse, where, all day long, numbers of people flocked, attracted by curiosity, or impelled by fears that missing friends or relatives might be found among the dead. The excitement was great, yet for some mysterious reason, not as absorbing as that of the nitro-glycerine explosion, although the present calamity involved a greater number of victims. After the explosion at Wells, Fargo & Co.'s, the streets were fairly blocked up by the crowd; to-day, although the occurrence took place within a hundred feet of Montgomery street, the tide of pedestrians ebbed and flowed past the little street which held this hecatomb with but a few idlers lounging on its corner. Californians are wonderfully adaptive, adjusting themselves to circumstances without confusion, and this second calamity was treated as a familiar episode.

Some of the incidents were singular. The first man taken from the building, was found wandering on the roof in his shirt, comparatively uninjured, but utterly bewildered and helpless. Another, who was rescued without a scratch, was awakened by hearing the walls crack, arose, dressed himself, examined the wall, and finding his suspicions verified, aroused several of the inmates, and passed into the street to examine the wall from the outside, as the building fell. The idea of an earthquake was impressed on many; one who was rescued described the sensation as similar; and added that when the building came down, he supposed that the destruction of the whole city was involved in that tremendous shock, and was only satisfied of his mistake, when a moment afterward he was seized and dragged from the ruins. The proprietor of the house, Mr Brewster, was killed by returning after the first alarm to rouse his lodgers; his wife, who also came back to bring away some article from her room, was badly bruised. Nearly all of the parties rescued alive, as well as the bodies of the dead, were partially clad, as if the whole household were preparing to speedily evacuate the premises. Some had barely time to get on their pantaloons, while the body of one man had on pantaloons and one boot. One man, who was asleep in third story of the building when it came down, was rescued in his night-shirt, and upon reaching the street was so completely bewildered that it was some minutes before he recovered his speech or senses. He turned about to re-enter the house, but upon looking up and not seeing it, he put his hands to his face and apparently gave up the problem in despair.

Nor were acts of quiet self-sacrifice and heroism wanting among the sufferers. Willie McCready, since dead, (son of the unfortunate man, whose name stands among the list of those killed instantly,) though bruised and bleeding, besought his rescuers to leave him and return for his father. Young Whittier, brother of Gen Whittier of the army, who had himself been four years in the service, exhibited great nerve and coolness. With his side horribly mangled so that the interior organs were exposed, he kept exhorting his fellow-sufferers to firmness and patience. Only when his wounds were being dressed did he utter a complaint; and then only that it was hard for a soldier who had braved death in the service of his country to die at last in such a way. Poor fellow! To have escaped the Wilderness and Petersburg for a mangled ending in San Francisco; to have dodged shot and shell to be done to death by bricks and mortar; to have survived unscathed the malignity of warfare to be the victim of one of the blunders and crimes of peace.

The direct cause of the accident was the excavation of an adjoining lot by parties who were building. The contractor had dug down some four or five feet below the wall of the Summer Street House, but fearing an accident from the superincumbent weight had notified the owner of the building of the danger. The owner referred the matter to his agent, who happened to be also a member of the board of supervisors. This agent and supervisor in his double capacity as a municipal sage and business man, examined the building and announced that it was safe. On the day before the accident, the contractor again ventured to call the agent's attention to the danger, but without success. The contractor advised shoring up the walls as a precautionary measure, but municipal wisdom did not think it necessary. In spite, however, of this half-authoritative decision, the building, as will be seen, fell, as it were, in direct opposition to municipal opinion and business forethought. Whatever be the verdict of the jury, whatever the theory of the press, criminal carelessness was the cause and sole agency of this dreadful calamity. Within the last three or four months, several buildings have fallen in different parts of the city, having been undermined, and their foundations sapped, through the same reprehensible carelessness. As they chanced to have been empty at the time, or the accident was confined to the broken limbs of one or two workmen, nothing has been said. The accident of to-day is the logical sequence of this recklessness of life and limb. The people are beginning to realize that there is something wrong. A morning paper, the Call, is very plain spoken, and I venture to borrow, as well as indorse, its editorial:—

Of course, hitherto nobody has been to blame for the reckless disregard of life and limb usually manifested by contractors and builders throughout the city. The results of man's wickedness and carelessness have been charged to Providential dispensations. Humanity has quietly shifted the burdens of its shortcomings and neglects to the shoulders of the Almighty. If an inoffensive man carries a harmless pistol in his pocket, he is punished for having something in his possession that might possibly destroy the life of a man; but if a lazy or incompetent contractor, or a penurious owner, undermines the walls of a four-story building so as to endanger their safety, or cause them to fall and break, bruise, or crush the bodies of citizens, he is held guiltless of all wrong doing. Yesterday morning, eight or ten lives were lost, and twice as many individuals maimed and bruised, by the wicked carelessness and criminal neglect of contractors or builders. This last catastrophe should arouse the authorities to the necessity of putting an end to the trifling with life heretofore practised by contractors and builders in this city. The guilty ones should be sought out and punished, no matter who they may be —whether owners, contractors or supervisors, who declare "no danger exists." What sense is there in sending men to prison for carrying little dirks or pistols in their pockets, and allowing contractors and others, whose carelessness causes numerous deaths, to go unscathed? During the last year, four times as many people in this city have been killed and maimed by the wicked neglect and carelessness of those engaged in building, as by the knife, pistol or bludgeon. Is human life of no value to this community, that reckless builders can be allowed to trifle with and take it with impunity? Is it any greater crime to kill one man with a pistol than it is to undermine the walls of a house and thus kill a dozen? Somebody is responsible—criminally responsible—for the Summer street tragedy, which has sent half a score of souls into eternity. If the authorities fail to fix that responsibility, they will be derelict in their duties. F.B.H.

LETTER 17

Christian Register, 15 September 1866

[From Our Regular Correspondent.]

CALIFORNIA.

San Francisco, Aug. 18, 1866.

You will have learned, by telegraph, before this reaches you, of the terrible accident and loss of life occasioned by the falling of a building in the most populous portion of our city yesterday, and the mail to-day takes the full details of the sickening catastrophe. But you will fail to get an idea of its moral effect, or the dangerous principle it illustrates, from these details alone.

One would think that criminal carelessness and reckless disregard of human life were sufficiently established as a feature of Western

civilization without this latest demonstration. The accident of yesterday was a logical sequence of the habits peculiar to communities like
ours. You can scarcely take up a paper without finding some record
of death or injury solely resulting from carelessness or negligence.
The lives sacrificed through these causes outnumbers the victims of
crime, disease or pestilence. Malignity has slain its tens, recklessness
its hundreds. The mortuary record of this State is two-thirds made up
of men who have blundered into death through their own or others'
negligence. Whether it be the wrecking of an ocean steamer, the boiler
explosion of a river boat, the falling of a building, like the tragedy
of yesterday, or the loss of life and limb through runaway horses,
carelessness is at the bottom of all. It is no extravagance to say that
nine-tenths of the accidents which occur, *ordinary* prudence and forethought could have prevented. Californians are a nation of gamblers
—taking chances ever as the regular operations of natural laws; specu-
lating even upon the merciful interventions of Providence. We are
whirled over our mountain roads, gallopping down declivities where
Eastern drivers would walk their horses and lock their wheels; we race
with the opposition steamboat, with a rag stopping yesterday's leak in
the boilers; we live in shells, erected over night like Aladdin's palace
and as likely to disappear, as if by enchantment, at the first earthquake; we drive half-broken horses with a free rein, or leave them
standing unhitched before our doors; our milkmaids milk cows but
one remove from the vicious wild cattle of the Spanish rancho, and
our tourist and pleasure-seekers risk their lives in picnics at inacces-
sible mountains and precipitous canons. But that a special Providence
looks after this impulsive people, we should soon be depopulated. To
repeat the idea I advanced a dozen lines above in its local and more
concrete form, we "gamble" a good deal in special providences and
"travel" on God's goodness.

The immediate cause of the accident of yesterday was the undermin-
ing of a building by some workmen who were laying the foundation
of another house beside it. The contractor becoming alarmed, and
having a professional respect for the theory of gravitation, notified
the agent of the threatened house. Thereupon, that gentleman twice
examined the wall, and assumed the risk that it would not fall. But
nature, for some unexplained cause, refused, in this instance, to sus-
pend her natural laws, and the house fell, with what result we know.
The risk undertaken by the agent was no greater than those assumed

here every day by contractors and builders. Three or four buildings have fallen from the same cause within as many months. Any one who chose, within the last fortnight, to walk along the line of the Kearney-street improvements, would have seen exhibitions quite as dangerous.

The Utopia of this coast—the place where the wind doesn't blow and fogs come not—has at last been found! This enchanted spot, this Xanadu of the San Francisco poetical dream, is situated about four miles from Oakland, on the opposite side of the bay, and is called "Berkeley." It is the college of California who have thus complimented the old bishop, and discovered in their homestead lands the great desideratum of this Pacific coast. They have just received a report from Fred. Law Olmstead, who visited the locality before leaving for the East, and who now sends them a plan (Central-Park-wise) for the laying out of their grounds, and bears testimony to the peculiar virtues of the place. If his opinion is to be believed it is certainly the Eden of this coast. Lying on an elevated plateau among the foot hills of the coast-range, it overlooks Oakland, San Francisco, the bay, and the ocean beyond. An unfailing stream of water irrigates its gentle slopes in the dryest of the dry season; trees, not yet twisted out of their natural curves of beauty by continued gales, spread their green crowns beneath an unclouded sky; evergreen lawns offer a perpetual carpet for the feet. The visitor, leaving behind him those bitter westerly gales of San Francisco, which relentlessly pursue him across the bay even to the confines of Oakland, arrives at Berkeley, to be lapped in Lybian airs, and to see his old enemy below him, tossing the waters of the bay, or wrestling with the thorny oaks of Oakland, but incapable of violating his retreat. He sees the afternoon fogs stealthily encircling the grey sand-hills of San Francisco with their white wreaths until the long line of streets are hidden from view, and above him arches the clear blue sky, (not the leaden, india-ink-washed firmament he left behind) while the sun, going down in a bank of fog sends its last level beams expressly to gild the serene charms of Berkeley. At night the stars beam with a peculiarly mild lustre; there is not wind enough to move the "curl from beauty's cheek," and, as most of our enjoyments here below are heightened by contrast, he lies down under the whispering boughs and thinks of his San Francisco friends huddled about their fires, and of the wind-swept and deserted streets of the Metropolis, and becoming convinced of the existence of a Great First Cause, he blesses Berkeley. At least, this is the evidence of Mr. Olmstead, endorsed by the trustees; if I have been led into unconscious poetry in dwelling upon Berkeley's charms they are to blame.

There is much intellectual life and activity in this community, but there is little opportunity for absorption. Our best men are giving out all the time without getting anything back in kind. A loneliness invest our few thinkers; there is so little intercommunication; so little emulation; so little active opposition or suggestion in the world of thought. I mention this more particularly in its reference to the few ministers of Liberal Christianity whose destinies have been cast on this shore. It was this isolation which gnawed at the vitality of King, and fettered the impulses of his broad Catholic spirit; it is this enforced seclusion from the broader sphere of an older civilization, with all its suggestions, aggressions, and varied aspects, which now eats like a lichen upon even such a granite nature as that of Stebbins. Consider this when you meet in fellowship and council—in convention and assembly—at the Eastern borders of the continent; try what can be done in mitigation of their loneliness, and think more tenderly of these unrelieved sentinels at the Western gate.   H.

LETTER 18

Christian Register, 29 September 1866

[From our Regular Correspondent.]

CALIFORNIA.

San Francisco, Aug. 30, 1866.

The sea, which is the Hygean goddess of San Francisco, has been subjecting us to heroic treatment for the ills peculiar to this epidemic season. Our population have been put through the packing process, and the wet fog-blankets are still hanging from the outer walls. In fact, the weather is a little overdone, as is everything in this queer climate. True, we have no summer complaints, such as cholera-morbus, dysentery, etc., but rejoice in colds, catarrhs and neuralgia in the middle of August. The evenings are frightful; the mornings little better. The streets are deserted by ladies, for the humid atmosphere takes the starch out of all calico, and even *moire-antique* relaxes its stiffness. Artificial flowers droop naturally from gay summer bonnets. Canaries pine in cages and forget to sing; the "daughters of music are brought low;" the "grinders cease because they are few," and select melodies from "*Il Trovatore*" are no longer slowly ground out at the street corners in the hours of ghostly twilight. On opera nights, however, when the city awakens to the flash of flickering gaslight, and, standing on Telegraph Hill, you can fancy the firmament that you miss above spread out below you, through the long twinkling parallelograms; opera cloaks and spotless nubias hurry by, and the dress-circles and parquets of theatre and opera come out with the retarded fashions of summer, and bloom with their polytinted glories. No unpropitiousness of weather or event can keep this mercurial people from their excitements or pleasures. If an earthquake were to shake down the town to-morrow, the ruins would be placarded the next day with an announcement of the early re-opening of theatre and opera house.

We have lately had a sensation in the shape of a Bloomer. Unfortunately for the woman who essayed this difficult *role*, the population did not take kindly to this product of an older civilization and progressive ideas, and she was followed through the streets by a mob of half-grown boys, and finally arrested. Luckily for the credit of the city, after being committed by the police judge, she was released on a *habeas corpus* before another magistrate, who failed to appreciate the legality of any municipal ordinance regulating a woman's dress. The more sensible portion of the community recognized the abstract justice of this decision, although they expressed no sympathy for the offender, whose conduct before and since certainly exhibited no higher purpose than notoriety and the reputation for martyrdom that she acquired. I do not think she made many converts in the community, and perhaps it is well for our social condition and prospects that she did not. Our society is too material in tone already; we cannot afford to accept any innovation which tends to lower the standard of female modesty, —to make her more masculine and confident. There is already too great lack of feminism, bashfulness, exclusiveness and timidity in our women, and California cannot countenance any theory, the effect of which is to broaden the sphere of female action at the expense of the home and social circle. There are too few *homes* here now. There is too great lack of such orthodox institutions as mothers and wives, to exchange them for feminine reformers and prophets.

The Church of England, in the Sandwich Islands, does not seem to prosper. You probably remember that it is also the Established Church of the Hawaiian Court, and that the English Bishop (Staley) its organizer, and head and front, has waged fierce warfare with the American dissenting missionaries, as well as the Episcopal, ever since he first came there and converted the imbecile king to what is now called the "Royal Hawaiian Established Reformed Catholic Church." This remarkable establishment is thus described by "Mark Twain," a genial humorist, as well as a thoughtful and discriminating observer, who has lately visited the islands:—

I will say a word or two about the Reformed Catholic Church, to the end that strangers may understand its character. Briefly, then, it is a miraculous invention. One might worship this strange production itself without breaking the first commandment, for there is nothing like it in the heavens above or in the earth beneath, or in the water under the earth. The Catholics refuse to accept it as Catholic, the Episcopalians deny that it is the church they are accustomed to, and of course the Puritans claim no kindred with it. It is called a child of the Established Church of England, but it resembles its parent in few particulars. It has got an altar which is gay with fiery velvet, showy white trimmings, vases of flowers and other mantel ornaments. (It was once flanked by imposing, seven-branched candlesticks, but these were obnoxious and have been removed.) Over it is a thing like a gilt signboard, on which is rudely painted two processions—four personages in each—marching solemnly and in single file toward the crucified Savior in the centre, and bringing their baggage with them. The design of it is a secret known only to the artist and his Maker. Near the pulpit is a red-canopied shower-bath— I mean it looks like one—upon which is inscribed, "Separated unto the Gospel of God." The bishop sits under it at a small desk, when he has got nothing particular to do. The organ pipes are colored with a groundwork of blue, which is covered all over with a flower-work wrought in other colors. Judging by its striking homeliness, I should say that the artist of the altar-piece had labored here also.

. . . A dozen acolytes, Chinese, Kanaka, and half white boys, arrayed in white robes, hold positions near the altar, and during

the early part of the service they sing and go through some performances suggestive of the regular Catholic services; after that,
the majority of the boys go off on furlough. The bishop reads a
chapter from the Bible; then the organist leaves his instrument
and sings a litany peculiar to this church, and not to be heard
elsewhere; there is nothing stirring or incendiary about his mild,
nasal music; the congregation join the chorus; after this a third
clergyman preaches the sermon; these three ecclesiastics all wear
white surplices. I have described the evening services. When the
bishop first came here he indulged in a good deal of showy display and ceremony in his church, but these proved so distasteful,
even to Episcopalians, that he shortly modified them very much.

The portrait of Bishop Staley, drawn by the same hand, is equally
incisive and pitiless, but its fidelity is corroborated by the statements
of most of the intelligent islanders:—

He gossips habitually; he lacks the common wisdom to keep
still, that deadly enemy of man, his own tongue; he says ill-advised
things in public speeches, and then in other public speeches denies that he ever said them; he shows spite, a trait which is not
allied to greatness; he is fond of rushing into print, like mediocrity the world over, and is vainer of being my Lord Bishop over
a diocese of fifteen thousand men and women (albeit they belong to other people's churches) than some other men would be
of wielding the world-wide power of the Pope; and finally, every
single important act of his administration has evinced a lack of
sagacity and an unripeness of judgment which might be forgiven
a youth, but not a full-grown man—or, if that seems too severe,
which might be forgiven a restless, visionary nobody, but not a
bishop. My estimate of Bishop Staley may be a wrong one, but it
is at least an honest one.

Persons who are intimate with Bishop Staley say he is a good
man, and a well-educated one, and that in social life he is com-
panionable, pleasant and liberal-spirited when church matters
are not the topic of conversation. This is no doubt true; but it
is my province to speak of him in his official, not in his private
capacity. He has shown the temerity of an incautious, inexperienced and immature judgment in rushing in here fresh from the
heart and home of a high English civilization and throwing down
the gauntlet of defiance before a band of stern, tenacious, un-

yielding, tireless, industrious, devoted old Puritan knights who have seen forty years of missionary service; whose time was never fooled away in theorizing; but whose lightest acts always meant business; who landed here two score years ago, full of that fervent zeal and resistless determination inherited from their Pilgrim forefathers, and marched forth and seized upon this people with a grip of iron, and infused into their being, wrought into their very natures, the spirit of democracy and the religious enthusiasm that animated themselves; whose grip is still upon the race and can never be loosened till they, of their own free will and accord, shall relax it. He showed a marvellous temerity—one weak, inexperienced man against a host of drilled and hardy veterans; and among them great men—men who would be great in wider and broader spheres than that they have chosen here. He miscalculated the force, the confidence, the determination of the Puritan spirit which subdued America, and underlies her whole religious fabric to-day—which has subdued these islanders, and whose influence over them can never be unseated.

LETTER 19

Springfield Republican, 1 October 1866
Springfield Weekly Republican, 6 October 1866

FROM SAN FRANCISCO.

Summer Weather on the Pacific Coast—Swill-Milk—The Summer Street
Catastrophe—Naughty Newspapers.

[From Our Special Correspondent.]

San Francisco, August 31, 1866.

Looking over the latest copy of The Republican received by mail, I begin to recognize a certain fitness in your having a representative from this coast among your correspondents. I can at least offer a relief to the monotony of their meteorological observations. While they, along the Atlantic seaboard, sing an unvarying "song of heat," and bear equal testimony to scorching skies, shades that are grateful, and brooks whose murmur the sultry atmosphere makes delicious, perhaps it is well that you have on this Pacific slope an exception to that isothermal crew—one sternly truthful and sadly sincere man, who can, out of his own experience, paint the opposite of that evenly charming picture; who could if he liked literally throw a wet blanket over their bucolic efforts. And yet I envy them. I have lingered at "Braeside" (can there be such a place?—the name is suspiciously imaginative) with "F.H.C.," until I have become penetrated with an abiding sense of its rural beauty, have smelt the "new mown hay"—alas, odorless here —"fragrant ferns and balsamic pines" of that rural solitude; I have rambled on Boston common with "Raynesford" until I have felt the old thrill which, as a boy (albeit not a native), I experienced when I first trod its green slopes and dipped my bare feet in its classic frog pond; I have sailed the "blue Vesuvian bay" with my fair countrywoman, Over the Seas, and at last awakened from this midsummer's night's dream to hear the wind hurrying past my window, in that fierce unrest peculiar to our California zephyrs, to see the thick fog mantling earth and sky, and poked my fire again in impotent longing. And yet I can imagine, if this material climate will permit such a vivid burst of fancy, that the genius of California, pictorially represented as a breast-plated, aggressive looking young woman, rebukes me sternly for my disloyalty. Where else can one so perfectly fulfill the real conditions of existence —eating, drinking, sleeping and working—as here?

Ought I not to be thankful that I can sleep under blankets instead of being driven to the necessity of celestial contemplation from an open window, through the extreme heat of a summer's night? Should I not be satisfied that I can work the summer through without needing vacation, instead of idling away a month or two in dreaming by babbling brooks or under whispering trees? Or, food being the question, I am pointed to the market, where Pomona has, in the reckless fashion in which everything is done here, poured out her stores in golden and purple grapes, nectarines, apricots and peaches, apples, pears and quinces, which heap the stalls in this damp, grey, autumnal weather. And here are watermelons! Watermelons, and the fog enveloping you like a wet sheet. Watermelons on your table, and a fire in your dining-room. Nature revolts and the blood curdles at the thought.

Let me be generous. We have had two days of clear weather, and the winds comparatively unobjectionable. But let me also be just. An old resident answered my congratulations with a dubious shake of the head, "Earthquake weather!" Nothing I can say here can equal this unconscious satire on the San Francisco climate. To be forced to look upon a fine day as abnormal and ominous, and to apprehend compensation in a general convulsion of the earth's surface, reveals a condition of things that even in my bitterest moments I have never yet ventured to express.

Bounteous as is nature's provision for the wants of this people, some of them are calling in art to extend the quantity of her offerings. The city's milk is watered; our suburban dairy cows are fed on swill. If in borrowing the pump and distillery for this purpose we have approximated to the civilization of older cities, we had much better kept to our original barbaric methods. The effect has been most alarming. The present mortality among young children is said to be owing to this poisoning of their nourishment. Even among adults we hear of cholera morbus, dysentery, and other disorders of the stomach, otherwise comparatively unknown and never epidemic in this city. Strangers are exempt. New York and Boston stomachs take more kindly to the adulterated stuff.

Young Whittier, who was supposed to be mortally injured in the Summer street catastrophe, is in a fair way to recover. His convalescence is almost miraculous, considering the extent and nature of his injuries. When first taken from the ruins his side was crushed in so that the viscera was exposed, his lungs were perforated by the broken fragments of his ribs, and yet he lives, and is expected with careful nursing to soon be upon his legs again. The case has attracted considerable attention among medical men. There have been no deaths among the wounded since the list I sent you on the 20th inst. The verdict of the coroner's jury is an artistic bit of whitewashing. They inveigh against abstract carelessness, but acquit the agent of the fallen building of any criminal neglect. As a specimen of "Crowner's quest law," I am strongly tempted to give you the two concluding paragraphs of the verdict:—

"And, from the above facts, the jury arrive at the conclusion that the fall of said building was caused by an excavation having been made parallel with, and two feet ten inches distant from, its eastern wall; that said wall, under these circumstances, reposed upon a clay bank, inadequate to sustain the pressure of so great a weight; that in the eyes of casual observers, as well as of practical mechanics, it was evident before the building fell that while there was no moral certainty, there was at least a probability that the wall might give way; that while such a probability existed, however faint it might be, it became the duty of the owner of said building, and likewise of those having made the excavation adjoining it, to take the necessary precautions to guard others against the smallest possibility of accident, as it apparently on one side involved the lives of tenants, and on the other of laboring men. They further conclude, and are of opinion, that while no one should perhaps be charged with criminal neglect, there was at least a want of due care exhibited on the part of those whose duty it was to see that proper measures be taken to prevent the happening of this terrible calamity."

The last sentence, considered as a *sequitur* to the previous one, is a bit of logic worthy of the gravedigger's comments on "crowner's quest law," in Hamlet. The grand jury have also added their wisdom to the preceding, but without going any further than some general and severe reflections upon gravitation.

A certain disreputable weekly, whose very title had become a suggestive synonym for indecent and reckless exposure, was lately indicted. Its circulation was confined to low saloons and groggeries—its readers to the frequenters of such places. The indictment was acceptable to the people generally, not excepting the readers of the sheet in question, for it is the fate of such literature to find few friends or apologists even among those who contribute to its support. The natural tendency of any exhibition of this nature being to intensify and highten its peculiar specialty as the morbid appetites of readers become sated, it was only a question of time when it would reach that point where the law could arrest it. That point was in fact reached some weeks before legal measures were taken, but for some reason the policemen who exhibited such zeal in arresting vendors of obscene prints and photographs, whose trade was carried on at least with some show of secrecy and deference to public opinion, permitted the flaunting exhibition in the public streets, on the news stands, of this weekly containing illustrations equally vile and offensive.

The disposition to pander to a vitiated taste is by no means confined to the extreme case just given. A newspaper published in this state, of considerable influence and extensive circulation, exercises an ingenuity worthy of a better cause, and exerts the whole force of its vast resources, to collate from eastern exchanges the most repulsive and disgusting details of outrage, rape and seduction. Day after day, the overland mail brings fresh matter, and a regular succession of crimes and outrages marshal themselves before the reader's eye like the ghosts in Macbeth. This is not the result of chance or accident any more than the procession of the seasons. There is an esthetic supervision of these things which betrays the hand of the connoisseur in *causes celebres*—the true artist in criminal reporting. A few years ago a correspondent of that paper, writing from New York, made a reputation upon the purely equivocal details of his letters. Scandal in private life, ambiguous incidents and domestic infidelities rehearsed in readable English, made up his spicy gossip. *Double entendre* and sly innuendo lent a fascinating charm to his pages. Like Vivien, he let his tongue "rage like a fire among the noblest names, defaming and defacing." Yet he simply achieved in clear English, on a higher plane, what the proprietor of the journal recently indicted is punished for clumsily executing in pot-house slang, in a lower sphere of life and society. Another paper here is made popular by the sparkling pruriency of an eastern correspondent who writes over a feminine signature. And yet this quasi-indecent, sensational literature is relished by people who also relish the sensational prudery of the Round Table, and who think they are virtuous, because they are willing to accept its statement that "Griffith Gaunt" is a naughty novel, and that our fashionable mothers and wives are drunkards.   F.B.H.

LETTER 20

Springfield Republican, 10 October 1866
Springfield Weekly Republican, 13 October 1866

FROM CALIFORNIA.

The City Election in San Francisco—Democrats in California—The Pacific
Board of Brokers Dissolved—The Epoch of Speculation—Ascent of Mount
Hood—Another Wonderful Discovery.

[From Our Special Correspondent.]

San Francisco, September 9, 1866.

The municipal election on the 5th inst. resulted in the triumph of the
Union party over an opposition who still adhered tenaciously to the old
democratic name and formulæ. Although only a municipal contest, in
which some of the later political issues mingled, it was also considered
a triumph over the new organization, reconstructed from the fossils
of the old chivalry, like Cuvier's Palaeotherium. It was supported by
organs that praise Andrew Johnson and Jefferson Davis in one breath.
It flew the title of "Union democratic" over a ticket made up of names
that were candidates under tickets headed by Breckinridge in '60
and McClellan in '64. It was specially unpalatable to the people from
the fact that most of its candidates for school directors were ignorant
Irishmen, of copperhead and anti-free school tendencies.

I notice a statement in some of your eastern journals to the effect
that San Francisco is a copperhead city. Nothing could be more unfair
and untrue. San Francisco is the loyal center of a loyal state, and since
the uprising of '61 has always thrown its vote on the side of Union and
republican principles. Thomas Starr King himself confessed that he
had been cheered for ultra sentiments, at the beginning of the struggle
which he would hardly have hazarded in any other city, not excepting
Boston. If the statement in regard to San Francisco copperheadism be
based on the usual conception of the politics of a large commercial and
cosmopolitan city, it is a mistake; if based on the actions of the 4th of

July committee in excluding negroes from the procession, it is a blunder, which arises from confounding the action of a few irresponsible and unrepresentative men, with the sentiments of an entire people.

Before dismissing politics let me say that the democracy here are terribly old-fogyish—and at least 6 years behind the age. They still rehearse old formulæ; talk about "nigger stealers," "abolitionists," and otherwise reiterate old epithets, so well worn that they might be retired from active service by act of Congress, as it was once proposed to restrict certain quotations by act of parliament. Rip Van Winkle, awakened from his long nap, harrahing for his Majesty King George, did not exhibit a more incongruous and ridiculous spectacle than these men who seem to have hibernated during the war. John Brown and his Virginia raid are still themes they harp upon; the "Resolutions of '98," Jefferson's maxims, and other *disjecta membra democratiæ* are things they still conjure with. That such an effete, decayed and thoroughly disintegrated organization as is the democratic party on this coast could affect our political integrity is simply ridiculous. It is in fact already dead, and only galvanized into spasmodic motion, now and then.

The Pacific board of brokers met the other day and quietly dissolved their organization. This may seem trifling news to chronicle, but is is an event of significant and momentous importance to the country. It meant that the reign of stock gambling was over; that bubble prices had been pricked, and fictitious values exploded; that business was once more settling down to a substantial basis, and finding its legitimate channels. The Pacific board of brokers was called into existence during the stock excitement of '64 as a rival of the San Francisco board. Here, stocks which had no value beyond the artistic beauty of their prettily printed certificates, shares of mines not yet opened and often not yet discovered, were bandied about at enormous but hypothetical figures. Here sharpers found their dupes, or "diamond cut diamond." Over its desk, now tenantless, were lost hard-earned fortunes, and often harder-earned reputations, the savings of poor men, the integrity of clerks and employes. On its walls were the prospectus of the "Dedbilgæ G. & S. Mining Company," and plots of land as intangible as Xanadu, or the Valley of Diamonds. Turn back to Irving's paper on the Great Mississippi Bubble, and you have a faint idea of the exciting scenes of '64. Companies were incorporated at the rate of 40 or 50 per day, and the county clerks waxed fat upon the fees. Notices of incorporation meetings, assessments and delinquents (but seldom of dividends) filled the columns of the daily papers, until supplements had to be added. Nice young men found openings at fair salaries, with the contingency of fine stock-jobbing opportunities, as secretaries; superintendents were appointed to oversee mines whose office was as illusionary as that of the Adelantado of the Seven Cities. Every man you met was a president, every other one a trustee, and all stockholders. Your washerwomen had ten feet in the "Highflier," your office-boy held certificates for 50 shares of "Aladdin." Quotations to the amount of millions filled the stock list of the dailies. Everybody talked stock. It was the subject of conversation in parlor and kitchen, at ball and soiree. Your fair partner no longer uttered the novel remark that it was "so hot!" but told you that "Excelsior" was "going higher." Young couples, in corners, no longer quoted Byron and Moore, but the stock list, and exchanged, instead of rings and vows, certificates and transfers. There were fair boards of brokers at lunch parties, stock operations at the matinees, and in the very threshold of the temple, in place of those who "sell doves for sacrifice," feet were bargained for and disposed of.

The result might have been easily imagined. But there was no crash, no financial panic; the reaction was gradual, and, save one or two exceptions, the victims were principally men of moderate means and circumstances, and business centers were not shaken by their failure or ruin. At first the papers were charged with ominously long lists of delinquent assessments; this was followed by sales and sacrifices—if the reduction of fictitious figures could be called a sacrifice. Shares for which $300 and $400 were paid were sold to pay an assessment of $2.50. Stocks hitherto considered perfectly safe, fell $1000 and $2000 per share; some on which valuable dividends had been paid were depreciated to zero. People who supposed themselves wealthy, found themselves reduced to exceedingly small practical incomes. Alnaschar sat disconsolate beside his basket of broken glassware. Riches vanished; no one knew where or why. It is roughly estimated that over $20,000,000 evaporated thus mysteriously.

Such is the retrospect of that epoch which seems to be significantly closed by the dissolution of this broker's board. Unfortunately, during the excitement, the seeds of many crimes and defalcations were sown, not to speak of the small bankruptcies, whose causes have been assigned to loss of capital in stock. Most of the late embezzlements, defalcations and insolvent cases have been traced directly to stock gambling. Superintendents and agents, the willing tools of unscrupulous directors, profited by their education and defaulted in turn. Clerks and employes embezzled to pay assessments, hoping to make good their accounts when the stock should rise. A few weeks since the agent of one of our principal corporations, becoming involved in stock speculations, used his employer's money, and when disgrace was inevitable accepted suicide as the easiest way out of his difficulties; and but a day or two ago another clerk in the same firm, of hitherto irreproachable character, tripped through the same causes and was arrested.

Professor A. Wood, with a party of gentlemen, has lately ascended Mount Hood. His account, given before the academy of natural sciences, established the fact that Mount Hood really is a volcano, and, further, that it is the highest mountain in the United States, if not in North America—being about 17,600 feet. Says the professor:—

> The summit area is of very limited dimensions—a crescent in shape, half a mile in length, and from three to 50 feet in width. It is a fearful place, as it is the imminent brow of a precipice on the north, sheer down not less than a vertical mile of bare columnar rock. This hight is lifted so far above all other hights (except the four distant snow clad peaks to the north, and Mount Jefferson on the south) that the country beneath seemed depressed to a uniform level, and the horizon retreated to a distance of more than 200 miles, including nearly all Oregon and Washington territory. The sublimity and grandeur of that view I must leave to the imagination of the reader. A canon of enormous depth plungles down along the southeast flank and is filled in part by a glacier evidently in motion, and having below a very abrupt termination. Terminal and lateral moraines mark its course, and a torrent of water issues from beneath. While we delayed here an avalanche of rocks, an immense mass, started by the wind, thundered down the left wall of this canon several thousand feet, and its track was marked by a trail of white smoke. On the west side of the ancient crater, at the base of a vast craggy pinnacle of rocks (a portion of the ancient rim of the crater), is still an open abyss, whence issue constantly volumes of a strongly sulphurous smoke. That there is also heat there is evident from the immense

depression of the snow about this place—depressed not less than 1000 feet below the snows which fill to the brim other portions of the ancient crater.

Since the discovery of the "Pliocene skull" we have had several "vestiges of creation" fished up in different parts of the state to tax our credulity, more or less. The latest discovery is a pre-Adamite "sinker" of stone, found some distance below the surface, in the classical suburb of Oakland. In the minds of intelligent scientific persons, according to the Oakland News, there can be no doubt that a race of sagacious beings practiced the sports of Isaac Walton, and fished over waters where now stands the city of Oakland, not only long before the conquest of California by the Americans, but before Adam's migration, as given in the Mosaic cosmogony.   F.B.H.

LETTER 21

Christian Register Supplement, 13 October 1866

[From our Regular Correspondent.]

CALIFORNIA.

San Francisco, Sept. 11, 1866.

Yesterday was the sixteenth anniversary of the admission of California into the Union, and was suitably celebrated by the Association of California Pioneers with a banquet and oration. Otherwise there was no observation of the day, the people not being very enthusiastic on the topic, and having always tacitly shifted to the Pioneers the duty of commemorating the day. The orator has been generally a Pioneer, although an exception was made in the case of Dr. Bellows, a visitor, and Rev. Horatio Stebbins, then comparatively a stranger— two Unitarian clergymen. The present orator was John H. Dwinelle, who has written the "Colonial History of San Francisco," an argument in the celebrated Pueblo case, in which he was counsel, and, saving Randolph's "Outline of a History of California," the most interesting retrospect of this country. In his oration, Mr. Dwinelle took an eminently California view of the past and future of the Pacific coast; believed that God had ordained California for the Pioneers; and that the sending of Stevenson's regiment was one of a series of special providences. With a legal subtlety worthy the city's counsel in the Pueblo claim, he actually tracked back our title to California to Pope Alexander VI. In his gratitude to that providence which he recognized as holding prior possession even to the pope, he was particularly severe upon Pantheism, and scouted at some length the theory that man was only an excellently developed baboon, though what this had to do with the pioneers, beyond being generally complimentary, is not entirely plain. He was specially severe upon the "Vestiges of Creation," which he characterized as a most "shallow and unscientific work." His peroration contained the following bit of history and suggestion:—

San Francisco was founded by a colony of soldiers and settlers, who came up for that purpose from Monterey, overland and by sea; and immediately set about constructing a chapel at the Presidio, after which the following proceeding took place, as recorded by Father Palou, one of the missionary priests who belonged to the expedition:—

"We took formal possession of the Presidio on the SEVENTEENTH DAY OF SEPTEMBER, the anniversary of the impression of the wounds of our Father San Francisco, the patron of the Presidio and Mission. I said the first mass, and after blessing the sites (*despues del bendito*) the elevation and adoration of the Holy Cross, and the conclusion of the service with the *Te Deum*, the officers took formal possession in the name of our sovereign, with many discharges of cannon, both on sea and land, and the musketry of the soldiers."

THE SEVENTEENTH OF SEPTEMBER, A.D. 1776, MUST THEREFORE BE CONSIDERED THE DATE OF THE FOUNDATION OF SAN FRANCISCO.

Ten years from now San Francisco will have completed the hundredth year of her existence. In ten years most of us, under the ordinary providence of God, will be still living. Let us, then, go on the hundredth birthday of our beloved city, go up and celebrate it on the plain of the Presidio, where she was born; let us renew the solemn exercises by which the soil was consecrated to civilization. The blessing of Holy Mother Church will not hurt the most zealous Protestant among us. Let us rear mast-high, with full military honors, to be replaced with equal honor by that

of Mexico, which in its turn shall give place with great discharge
of musketry to our own national emblem of union and strength!

The society of Pioneers have been hitherto merely a club, devoted
to mutual admiration and self-perpetuation, whose duties begun and
ended with the enrollment of new members, or the payment of the last
tribute of respect to the memory of the old. Anybody who arrived here
in '49 or '50 was eligible. While this list includes some names really
creditable to the State, a majority of the men most instrumental in
building up the community were not eligible. The accident of priority
of residence was by no means indicative of worth. It must be remembered that the character and motives of our founders will not bear
close scrutiny. No wave of religious enthusiasm like that which preci-
pated the original settlers on the shores of New England, or carried
the cross of Spanish conquest over the plains of Mexico, brought the
pioneers to these shores; no industrial energy like that of the Western backwoodsman ever opened a way to our solitudes. The less said
about the motives of some of our pioneers the better; very many were
more concerned in getting away from where they were, than in going
to any particular place. But of late the usual vein of pioneer-eulogium
has been worked out; orators have gone back beyond the American
occupation for themes to admire; the labors of the missionaries have
been recognized; the nucleus of a historical society has been formed,
and the pioneers have done something better than a reference to '49
and '50.

On Sunday evening last, Rev. Horatio Stebbins preached upon "Revivals." I wish I could give you an outline of one of the best sermons
ever delivered in that pulpit, graced as it has been by King and Bellows; but I can do no better than merely echo the praises of his audience. He seems to steadily grow in favor—a liking so deliberately and
dispassionately formed as to be the basis of an enduring reputation
here. I think the people—I speak now of the world outside his church,
who know him only at benevolent meetings, patriotic and public celebrations—count upon him with a certain calm security, which your
simply brilliant man cannot produce; his appearance on the platform
always diffuses a comfortable warmth, without any feverish exaltation among the audience; there is a visible readjustment of attention
and reseating in anticipation, however late the hour or prolonged the
meeting. The modesty of his prefaces, the lack of declamatory tricks,

contribute much to this satisfaction, and his thorough earnestness, which gives as much vigor to his simplest statement as his finest figure, completes the conquest. His best thoughts seem to slip from him without inflection or emphasis; there is no note of warning to rouse the hearer into the attitude of expectancy. Thoroughly impressing you from the first with his vitality and earnestness, he carries you along with him more by the force of what he says, than *how* he says it; more through recognition of the truth than his occasional felicities of illustration, which in so many speakers has the effect of stopping-places where half the audience linger. He wins your attention, for you never know when he is going to say his best thing. His figures are rough-hewn granite, and when he is excited he thrums them out as Vesuvius does her scoria, hot, ponderous and glowing. In argument he is more given to straight-hitting from the shoulder than sparring.

In the church he has won his reputation through sheer momentum of character. When he first arrived the conditions were all against him. The remembrance of King's flashing genius and personal magnetism; the interregnum filled by Bellows in a half Episcopal capacity, scarcely prepared the congregation for the advent of a man who, at first sight, seemed so different from them. Their recollection of King was a poetic landscape, full of tender lights and shadows, with a foreground of vivid color and illimitable distances of snowy peaks; of Bellows a more modern picture, somewhat more pastoral, human and cultivated; while Stebbins, like all abstract thinkers, presented in his oratory and manner at first sight only those bleak Alpine solitudes where the purely intellectual dwell. But closer familiarity detected the exquisite atmospheric tints which invested this rocky nature; and the beauty and delicacy of lichen and moss, that covered it; that it had its varied charms from whatever position it was viewed; and that like Shasta or Mount Hood you always knew where to find it. And so the very ruggedness of his nature offered facilities for sympathy to cling to or climb by, and beginning by winning the respect, he seems to have at least attained the sincere love of his parish.

L E T T E R   2 2

Springfield Republican, 17 October 1866
Springfield Weekly Republican, 20 October 1866

FROM CALIFORNIA.

The State Fair, its Legitimate Attractions and Peculiar Side Shows—The
Watering Places—The Grave of a Pioneer Yankee Woman.

[From Our Special Correspondent.]

San Francisco, September 18, 1866.

The annual state fair at Sacramento closed on the 16th inst. The agricultural display was about equal to that of the preceding year. Among the manufactures exhibited was a piece of California made silk, placed beside the silk-worm, egg, and mulberry leaf—all of local culture— demonstrating that this was now a branch of California industry. I am inclined to think, however, that the public interest centered more in that noble animal, the horse, and that noblest of sports, horse racing. There were Durham, Devonshire and Ayrshire cattle, American cows and Merino sheep; but Norfolk (famous from his race with Lodi) led them all. What Californian could give his attention to the slow increase of stock-breeding and cattle-raising, with this opportunity for rapid returns from investments, so close at hand. But there were other opportunities for betting beside this comparatively respectable method. During the fair week the gambling hells were in full operation. Faro, monte and roulette were as openly played as in the palmy days of '49 and '50. The streets of the capital in fact exhibited all the lawlessness and license of that interesting epoch. The fair seems to have been an excuse for rascality of all kinds. The exhibition of "honest wares" from the rural districts was far inferior to the display of urban swindling and the games of city sharpers. The fattest Durham failed to draw the crowds that were attracted by the popular "tiger." Gangs of horse jockeys, fast men and dissolute rancheros congregated on street corners, and carriages filled with painted women occupied the race grounds. There were side shows which in vulgarity and coarseness equaled any English rustic game of the past century, with a certain California originality superadded. One, in particular, requires some ingenuity of polite periphrasis to describe. A stout woman in tights, artificially padded and cushioned over that part of her body where the bustle was formerly worn, stood in the center of a small circle. The game consisted in striking her upon the aforesaid cushion with a large mallet or beetle. If the blow was sufficiently powerful to force her out of the ring $3 was paid to the skillful player. The price of a "chance" was twenty-five cents. It hardly need to be said that the percentage was against the player, as the woman, with the characteristic obstinacy of her sex, resisted these forcible attempts to dislodge her, in most cases successfully. This eminently agricultural sport was exceedingly popular, appealing, as it did, in one breath, to the vulgarity and speculative tendencies of the crowd.

The display of "blooded stock"—I am speaking of the horses now —was very fine. There were the usual number of professional gentlemen, lounging by them, with wisps of straw in their mouths, possibly out of compliment to the animal, and a general flavor of horse pervading their clothes, their manners and their speech. They had the usual appearance of inferiority—of belonging to the particular animal they looked after. The blooded stock, on the other hand, suggested to you the idea that they harbored a contemptuous opinion of their masters, looking upon them as folk who could not trace their pedigree very far into the past without coming across ordinary farm stock, who used to say "Which?" for "How?" and sat down to dinner in their shirt sleeves, and did their courting on Saturday night. A few of the more spirited had a very suggestive way of lifting up their little, round hoofs now and then, and producing some excellent sheet-lightning imitations with the whites of their eyes.

Although our pleasant weather is just commencing—the few warm, humid days in September which prophesy the rainy season—the people are already returning from the different watering places. In the absence of any news I may as well say a few words about this kind of recreation. A California watering place is, in the first place, the natural climax of several inconsistencies. In a country where there is so much clear weather and so few pleasant days, where the "maiden spring wears an air of mature self-assertion, where April is sincere and June hypocritical, where the leafy shadows of July harbor rheumatism and the zephyrs of August are something to fly from," it is naturally difficult to fix upon any season suitable for vacation, or any locality as the proper place to enjoy it. But there are periods when the dried up denizens of the sere Sacramento valley encounter their chilly brothers of the Bay city as they go on their respective sanitary missions, when the Sacramentan exchanges his fever and ague for a bronchitis, and the San Franciscan gives up his rheumatism for a sun-stroke (as in Addison's vision). Yet they are mostly restricted in their choice of watering place to some hollow in the hills with a spring and hotel, smelling of new paint and sulphur. These places generally look alike, and a description of one will do for all.

There are long hotel corridors that the wind howls malevolently through; there are Swiss cottages with the eaves warped by the sun; there are gardens where roses flourish with perennial and prodigal luxuriance. There are youthful fruit trees, with fruit prematurely set, with scarce leaf enough to mantle their first matronly blushes. There are arbors and shaded seats for "whispering lovers made," but I fancy they chill the most ardent temperaments, for even with the fervid mid-day sun, the shadows always hide a lurking coolness. Perhaps this is the reason why most of the love-makings at these places are carried on in buggies and on horseback, disguised by rapid driving, and culmi-nating in proposals at the highest point of speed. Beyond the garden there are open meadows of wild oats and clover of a vivid green; but, although luxuriant in perspective, you find in strolling over that broad, odorless expanse, that the vegetation is sparse and thin, and the black, oleaginous earth quite visible to the eye, and always palpable to the foot, as though carpets, even with nature, were the products of an older civilization. But there are the clear stereoscopic outlines of distant hills, a tonic exhilaration in the dry, crisp air, and a certain wide-awake intensity in the sunlight.

The social aspects of these watering places are not unlike those of the East, although many of the peculiarities are intensified. Shoddy is here, and California shoddy at that. Sinbad the sailor stops here to spend "in festivity and merriment" the money obtained at the Valley of Diamonds. Washoe speculators, Montgomery street stockbrokers and "new men" come and go, as fortune fluctuates; the ruined man of yesterday making way for the lucky spendthrift of to-day. The simplest recreations being expensive, display is shown in fast horses, excessive wine and much billiards, and some objectionable brooches and bracelets. The ladies are comparatively inferior to the men, as they are throughout the entire state. Among the few unprotected but not unattended married women who frequent these places, there is, without perhaps any palpable breach of propriety, considerable trifling with trusts, which paves the way to that easy carelessness with which they are at last broken, which has made California so notorious. The divorced wife revels in her new freedom with a conscious grace that is the constant envy of those hapless women who are condemned by cruel fate to flirt up to the uncertain limit of a certain tether. Husbands and brothers have little time for recreation. You see them drive up to the hotel door in dusty buggies, drawn by dashing horses covered with foam, and bearing every evidence of having been furiously driven. They crowd a vast quantity of exciting detail into the narrow limits of their vacation, and call it repose and recreation. You see them at table and at the bar-room five minutes after they have arrived. They retire to the billiard table and exercise the ivory balls till midnight; they rise at 4 a.m. to fish in a neighboring trout stream, return to an early breakfast, harness their fine horses, and depart, as they came, in a cloud of dust.

There are, of course, happy family groups, but they are exceptional. The children are peculiar, ruddy-cheeked, sinewy youngsters, with high health brimming their quick eyes. They look charming at a distance, and you are generally inclined to let them remain there. If you look at them closely you will find among those of California birth certain indigenous qualities. The popular floral figure of youth would not apply to them with any fitness; there was no bud or blossom about them, perhaps because the native California flowers are themselves fragile, brilliant and ephemeral, but I often fancied I detected a coarseness of fiber and precocity of growth which belonged to a country of mammoth strawberries, and fruit-bearing trees only a foot high. Talking with them, you will find a readiness of expression and quick self-assertion which seems to be appropriate to a country where spring is born full grown, like Minerva. If you bestow a pat on the head and a half dollar to the tallest, you cannot help feeling a certain suspicion that the money will not be foolishly thrown away on cakes or taffy, but decently expended in an initiatory game of billiards, or laid away for a future investment.

Many of these popular watering places are new, and have been established to meet the exigencies of the public. But one I lately visited had something of a past history, and I took up my abode in an old adobe building which had been overlooked in the improvements, and which was used to accommodate an overplus of pleasure seekers. It had been originally built by a brother of the Mexican commandant at the time of the establishment of an adjacent military post, perhaps 80 years ago. It had been since occupied by a trapper of the Hudson Bay company, who, long before the American occupation, brought a Yankee wife hither, who died and was buried here. Although her grave must have been long since obliterated, I seldom pass through the garden without a vague expectation of stumbling upon it. I often found myself wondering if the monotony of her secluded life had hardened her nature, or if she ever shrunk from the dull eyes and barbaric faces that surrounded her. If she ever wearied of the unvarying succession of cloudless summer skies, or the dreary patter of the rain on the red tiles through the long wet season, or if she longed for the country where the snow mantle magically changed the landscape, and summer showers made it young again; or if, in some dim prophetic dream, she ever heard the far-off ripples of the rising tide of emigration, and knew that some day a fair faced countrywoman would stand beside her grave and say to the man who stood with her: "They say a Yankee woman was buried here, long ago. Poor thing! How horrid it must have been."   F.B.H.

LETTER 23

Christian Register, 27 October 1866

[From our Regular Correspondent.]

CALIFORNIA.

San Francisco, Sept. 28, 1866.

I have alluded in one of my previous letters to the English Church Establishment at the Sandwich Islands, and the conduct of its Bishop. In a letter to the *Pacific Churchman* the Bishop of California (Episcopal) denies the generally accepted statement that the appointment of Bishop Staley of Honolulu was a political movement to strengthen English influence at the Sandwich Islands. Bishop Kip states that the late W. C. Wyllie, Minister of Foreign Relations, wrote to him some years ago relative to the appointment of some American Episcopal clergyman, but that there were no clergymen to spare, and in spite of his (Bishop K.'s) repeated applications to the Domestic and Foreign Committees he received no encouragement. It was then, that, happening to visit England in 1860, he, at the request of Mr. Wyllie, made an arrangement with the English clergy, which resulted in the appointment of Bishop Staley as Missionary Bishop. "It was," says Bishop Kip, "agreed that it should be a *joint mission*—that two or three clergy should be sent out by the Church of England, and the same number by the American Church, when practicable. The *animus* of the whole affair was shown in a single remark made to me on this occasion by the Bishop of London—'I am happy,' said he, 'that the application for this mission comes from an American Bishop, so that it cannot be said that the Church of England is obtruding herself on the Islands.' This simple remark settles the whole point at issue which has since been made by the opponents of the mission."

Unfortunately this single remark does not settle the whole point at issue, nor any part thereof, except so far as it transfers the responsibility of foisting an absurd and ridiculous church establishment upon an unwilling people, from the English Church to the shoulders of an American Bishop. However sincere might have been his intention, he is placed, by his own showing, in the position of having appealed to the English Church, to assist him in displacing his own countrymen, from the foothold they had gained through many years' hard missionary labors—in overthrowing their work and the political prestige they had thus honorably obtained. The request of the late Mr. Wyllie was not the request of the people; it was simply the voicing of a few English sycophants of the court, who were alarmed at the quiet political influence gained by the American missionaries. The Minister of Foreign Relations knew that the American Episcopal Church on this coast carried no national or political influence with it, and could be used as he might wish to use it, when he addressed its Bishop. He succeeded better than he expected. He baited for a porpoise, but caught a whale. When the Domestic and Foreign Committee refused to interfere with the good work of their countrymen in the Islands, Bishop

Kip was too ready to make the appeal to the English clergy. Well might the Bishop of London be "happy" that the application "came from an American Bishop." What the English Ecclesiastics, in prudent courtesy, shrunk from attempting of themselves, the zeal of an American bigot, or the officiousness of an American "cream-cheese" made smooth to them. It is amusing that this disclosure is now made with a certain self-congratulatory air of meritorious service performed; while the allusions to a visit to "Fulham Palace," and other suggestions of intimacy with English nobility and high church dignitaries, show very plainly the *animus* of the whole proceeding—that weakness for titular dignity which has made this unfortunate prelate the butt of his own diocese.

Queen Emma, the dowager queen of those perhaps too-ecclesiastically-favored Islands, is now stopping with us. The people of this city have behaved towards her with courtesy and respect, without flunkeyism or loss of simple republican dignity; but the municipal authorities have shown themselves boors by omitting any formal civility or attention toward the lady who has lately been the guest of the nation, and to whom the Secretary of State has just offered, by telegraph, a passage home in the federal war-steamer, Vanderbilt. This little *contretemps* of course will be used as capital by the enemies to California interests in the Islands.

The Rev. Mr. Ames is at Sta. Cruz, sandwiched between the eternal pines and the eternal ocean. He is there (temporarily I believe) for his health's sake, for which he returns compensation by exercising a spiritual sanitary supervision over this charming watering place. He preaches every Sunday, and could, if he chose, make the engagement a permanent one, for he is much loved by the more cultivated residents and visitors, who are both able and willing to put their regard into the form of an acceptable offer. Letters from Sacramento to the Pacific branch of the Liberal Society speak of him highly during his late visit, and dwell in sanguine terms on the prospect of speedily organizing a parish for him there.   H.

LETTER 24

Springfield Republican, 27 October 1866
Springfield Weekly Republican, 3 November 1866

FROM CALIFORNIA.

Queen Emma at San Francisco—A Shabby and Discourteous Reception—
The Limantour Fraud—More about California Stock Gambling.

[From Our Special Correspondent.]
San Francisco, September 29, 1866.

The royal standard of Hawaii floats from the tall flagstaff of the Occidental Hotel, where her majesty, Queen Emma, who arrived on the steamer a few days ago, holds her court. This is her last stopping place on her return to the islands, and, judging from the ovations she received in the East, the enthusiasm seems to have decreased as she nears home. Beyond the crowd of idlers, which a dog fight or any local excitement will collect in Montgomery street in five minutes, who assembled at the door of the hotel as she stepped from her carriage, there was little public interest felt; people transacted business, gambled in stocks, ate, drank and slept as unconcernedly as though royalty had not pitched its tents within the walls. As a general thing, Californians are not much affected by titles or position, at least not to the extent of older civilizations; there is very little toadying to place or office, and public sentiment runs rather to satire and skepticism than to tuft-hunting or toad-eating. Men and women pass for what they are worth from a California standard, which I need not say is remarkably elevated. Our conceit consequently is more apt to make us patronizing than obsequious. Recall the difference between the reception of the Japanese quasi-mercantile ambassadors in New York and San Francisco. Here these two-sworded, brocade-legged, amber-tinted diplomats, with the youthful "Tommy" over whom fair New York went crazy, passed and repassed through the streets hardly eliciting more remark than well dressed Chinamen. We have lords and bishops,

Indian chiefs and foreign dignitaries among us. We lay claim, as you probably know, to easy acquaintanceship with Grant, Sherman and indeed all the great men of the war, and did we not specially send Baker and Halleck? Do not distinguished travelers and tourists seek us out? have we not had Bayard Taylor, Bierstadt, Fitz Hugh Ludlow, Colfax, Greeley, Bellows, Bowles and Bross? Go to! Shall we debase ourselves before the dark-skinned queen of a neighboring island which we are only trifling with before we finally absorb, whose ports are important only as harbors for our whalers, whose canefields are fruitful only for our consumption, whose volcanoes are known and admired only through the description of our tourists?

Nevertheless it would have been more decent and respectful if the municipal authorities had taken some formal part in the reception. The mayor and supervisors did nothing, probably *mauvaise haute* of the jokes of their constituents, or from a difference of opinion with Mr Seward as to the respect due to a friendly power. It might have been expected that when the secretary of state chose to extend his hospitalities to Queen Emma, the mayor of San Francisco might have accepted it as a precedent. But it was otherwise. Except the saluting of the federal forts and war-ships and the courtesies of the collector, there was no formal reception. The municipal authorities did not go to the wharf, and the queen—a good-natured, amiable lady, whose instincts were sufficiently refined to notice the discourtesy—was received in solitary state, and conducted to her carriage and hotel by her consul, Mr Hitchcock of San Francisco. A graceful opportunity of showing some courtesy toward a people from whom we expect so much and to whom we have done so little, a nation that must sooner or later become identified with our own, was lost, by our ridiculous policy of entrusting the conduct of a great city to the hands of underbred and underpaid nobodies.

It is said that an occurrence as *mal adroit* and boorish as this lost us the friendship of the late king, who was ejected from a car in New York on account of his color by a too sensitive Celtic conductor. Queen Emma has considerable political power by virtue of her intelligence and experience, and the court is already committed to the Oxford-Coutts-Staley-Reformed-Catholic-Church-of-England *quasi* political establishment at Honolulu. The islanders are predisposed to like us and to hate the church, but they also have a superstitious love and loyalty for their king and the royal family, and it would have been at least politic, to leave courtesy out of the question, had we respected their instincts.

The famous or infamous Limantour fraud has lately been resurrected in our courts in another aspect. Every Californian is familiar with the history of this gigantic swindle, but as it may be new to some readers of The Republican, I may be pardoned for repeating it here. After the American occupation and discovery of gold, when San Francisco was a flourishing young city and property became valuable, the citizens were startled by the appearance of one Jose Y. Limantour, a Mexican, who coolly claimed not only almost the entire peninsula upon which the city is built, but all the islands in the bay, under grants from the Mexican government. When the question came before the courts, then inexperienced in the manner in which Mexican grants were manufactured, by dint of forgery and false swearing, the claim was actually established, it is said even to the astonishment of the claimant himself! Limantour at once became a millionaire. Limantour rapidly disposed of property here and there, or compromised with actual possessors at exorbitant sums. But, as he waxed wealthy, he grew more avaricious and grasping. The government wished to buy Alcatraces island as the site for a fortress, and offered a certain price to Limantour. He refused to sell except at an enormous sum. In vain the federal representatives endeavored to bargain; Limantour had fixed his compensation, he saw the government at his mercy, and he was inflexible. This decision was his ruin. Provoked at his exorbitance, the authorities began to question his title, hunted up testimony, and finally had the case re-opened. Overwhelming proof was now brought forward that the testimony on which his claim was founded was perjured, and that his documents were forged. The unlucky millionaire was tried and convicted of forgery and held to bail in the sum of seventy thousand dollars. He gave the bail and fled the country. Such is the history of the Limantour swindle, as far as that individual was personally concerned.

The subsequent history of the case may be briefly recounted, as follows: Limantour's bondsmen were Michael Reese and Manuel Cartro. It was supposed at the time that the bail would not be prosecuted, or if prosecuted would evade payment by some legal quibbling, and the case slept from 1856 till about a year ago. Then Cartro being insolvent, suit was commenced against Michael Reese, whose income last year was returned at about $100,000, and judgment given a few days ago for $35,000. The result was unexpected, and has given great satisfaction to the public, as a precedent against the custom of "straw bail," and as a culminating, though tardy, rebuke to all concerned in this great land swindle, which has been since imitated, at different times, with greater or less success.

In a previous letter I alluded to the gradual decay of stock gambling and its causes. In that connection I now offer a few facts which I condense from a good local authority. It will give eastern readers a faint idea how money has been squandered on this coast. Fifty-four mines which appear on the list of the board of brokers and have, in the aggregate, 125,216 shares of stock, have cost, in assessments, $6,900,872, or about $55 per share. If these stocks were disposed of at their present market value they would bring only $3,235,000, or about $25⅔ per share. Somebody has lost $3,664,942, and that somebody includes most of our people. The Savage, Yellow Jacket, Crown Point, Hale & Norcross, are included in this list, all looked upon as valuable mines. In the Washoe district 26 mines have cost in assessments $4,864,069, and their market value now is quoted at $3,235,930. In the Esmeralda district, 8 mines, costing $784,650, have their market value expressed by 0. In the Coso district, 3 mines, costing $140,750; in the Reese River district, 11 mines, costing $360,710; in the Humboldt district, 2 mines, costing $255,293, all have their values—or what they would realize to-day in the market—expressed by the same cipher. These lost riches have gone no one knows where; they have come mostly from the pockets of poor men; with them in many cases have flown self-respect, honor, happiness, and often life itself.　　　　　　　　　　F.B.H.

LETTER 25

Springfield Republican, 3 November 1866
Springfield Weekly Republican, 10 November 1866

FROM CALIFORNIA.

The Indian Summer of the Pacific Coast—Earthquakes—Steamboat
Explosion—Attentions to Queen Emma—A New Lecturer in the Field.

[From Our Special Correspondent.]

San Francisco, October 9, 1866.

We are enjoying our finest season—that tranquil interval between summer and winter, when the winds have ceased and the rains have not yet come. It might be our Indian summer; an Indian summer in etching only, without the filling in and coloring. There is no glory of painted woodland nor hazy distances, but sea and sky are exquisitely blue, and the farther mountains stand out in the calm, still air in stereoscopic outline. There is just enough warmth and humidity in the atmosphere to relieve it of that dry asperity which makes our summers so intolerable, not enough to create languor, or the dreamy abstraction that belongs to an eastern autumn day. It is a thin sentimental streak in this otherwise matter of fact, wide-awake climate. If nature ever had her moments of poetic weakness here, this would be her solitary idyl. Long days of soft yellow sunshine, very different from the high white and staring lights of our summer days, succeed each other at this season, fading into tender twilights and balmy evenings, when the constellations seem to be nearer, and the moon looks so kindly that we begin once more to believe in the story of Endymion, and it does not seem so ridiculous for any sane man to sleep in the open air, as it did. Summer relents at the last moment, and as she departs, gives us one glimpse of her chary beauties. I am perhaps over particular in describing the charms of this rare season, for I have been accused of vilely slandering the "finest climate in the world." Let this honest tribute to our last two weeks of lovely weather stand recorded against that charge.

Yesterday was the anniversary of the great earthquake shock of last year. There was no recurrence of the phenomena in California—the few tumblings we have felt this spring and summer hardly justifying the name. Further up the coast, however, they tell a different story. In Russian America, south-east of the peninsula of Alaska, there is an island called Kodiac. The ship Imperial, which arrived the other day, bringing ice to the Russian American commercial company, brought also the news of a frightful earthquake on that island, which, in conjunction with her cargo, sent a cold chill through the city. Three houses and every chimney in the town of St Paul were knocked down. The Imperial was lying in the harbor at the time, and her captain describes the sensations produced by the shock as frightful beyond description. The vessel appeared as though she was being dragged at railroad speed over the rocks. Huge masses of stone that had lain unmoved for centuries, were torn from their resting place on the mountain side and hurled with deafening noise to the bottom of the valleys below. Although great damage was done to property, no lives were lost. The Caroline E. Foote, whaling schooner, arrived a few days later at this port, and records that on the same day, in latitude 54.20 north and longitude 147.20 west, about one hundred miles southeast of Trinity Island, she experienced a violent earthquake shock. The vibration was from northwest to southeast, lasting nearly a minute, and immediately succeeded by another shock, but not so heavy nor of so long duration. The captain says that in 30 years experience he never met one of equal violence. It altered the rate of the chronometer 63 miles. After the shock, a smart breeze which had been blowing ceased, the sea fell, a calm succeeded, which was twenty minutes later followed by a hurricane which lasted 52 hours.

While we have been free from earthquakes, accidents are multiplying with us, and this year seems to be peculiarly fateful. The nitroglycerine explosion was followed by the Summer street catastrophe, and within the past few days the papers have been filled with the particulars of another frightful accident by which nine men have lost their lives. The steamboat Julia, plying between this city and Stockton, on the 29th ult., blew out the bottom of her steam drum when but a few miles from the wharf, scattering death and destruction among her crew. At the time of the explosion the deck hands of the boat were at dinner, between decks, near the door leading to the engine room, and were instantly enveloped in the rushing steam. They endeavored to escape by the forward deck, but the passage way was blocked up by two horses that were tied there. A few were killed instantly, others were taken out in the agonies of death, and some died after being removed to the hospital. None of the passengers were injured. The evidence elicited before the coroner's jury shows that the steam drum was discovered to be leaking about a quarter of an hour after the boat left the wharf, and that the attention of the captain was called to it by the engineer. The captain then ordered the boat about to return for repairs. She had scarcely turned her prow toward the city, when the explosion took place. Although the evidence of the engineer, captain and a few experts declare the accident to have been unavoidable, and that proper precaution was taken in turning the boat about, there is a strong opinion that this precaution was not enough; that the steam should have been blown off, and no attempt made to run the boat, in that dangerous condition, to the wharf. One paper says "the moment the engineer saw the escape of steam, he was cognizant of danger, but he still kept up steam and endeavored to run back to the landing. He was willing to take a risk of ten or fifteen minutes, but not a risk of ten or fifteen hours. But it saved trouble to run the boat back—hence the catastrophe occurred." The jury exonerated all parties concerned, much to the surprise of every one who has not studied the peculiar mental processes by which coroners' juries arrive at conclusions. Since the rendering of the verdict two more of the injured have died in hospital, giving a chance for another inquest and an opportunity for final justice. But it is not probable that anything will be done.

The story of the ill-fated ship Hornet, and the sufferings of her crew in their long voyage in an open boat, has been already told, and the world has been thrilled at the recital. The story is not yet complete. Samuel Ferguson, one of the survivors, who also kept a journal during that terrible voyage and calmly recorded each day's suffering until their final delivery, died a few days ago at Congress Springs, of disease superinduced by his exposure. His journal, edited by competent hands, is to be given to the eastern public soon. I have seen it, and know of nothing in literature which compares with its simple, graphic earnestness and unconscious pathos.

The Vanderbilt waits for Queen Emma, whose visit here is nearly concluded. Within the past ten days her majesty has received many courtesies from our prominent citizens and officials, visiting the principal places of interest in the city, and voyaging round our bay in the revenue cutter Shubrick, which the collector of the port placed at her disposal. A modest, unassuming and refined gentlewoman, she will doubtless appreciate the hospitality which Californians have extended to her without ostentation or affectation. With a genuine show of good feeling there has been no excitement, flunkeyism, mobbing, or exhibition of snobbery since her arrival here. She speaks in glowing terms of the courtesies she has received in the United States, and I hope has forgotten that her husband was ever insulted in our free country on account of his color. The short-comings of her first official reception here, I trust, have been also buried in oblivion.

Samuel Clemens, better known as "Mark Twain," the Honolulu correspondent of the Sacramento Union, took advantage of the interest attending the queen's visit to deliver a most entertaining lecture upon the Sandwich Islands. He had a crowded house and a brilliant success, and in this initial effort at once established his reputation as an eccentric lecturer whose humor surpassed Artemus Ward's, with the advantage of being a more legitimate quality. He had already acquired, here and abroad, considerable fame as an original and broadly humorous writer, but he took his audience by storm. He intends repeating the lecture through the state and is urged by his friends to extend his tour even to the East. His humor is peculiar to himself; if of any type, it is rather of the western character of ludicrous exaggeration and audacious statement, which perhaps is more thoroughly national and American than even the Yankee delineations of Lowell. His humor has more motive than that of Artemus Ward; he is something of a satirist, although his satire is not always subtle or refined. He has shrewdness and a certain hearty abhorrence of shams which will make his faculty serviceable to mankind. His talent is so well based that he can write seriously and well when he chooses, which is perhaps the best test of true humor. His faults are crudeness, coarseness, and an occasional Panurge-like plainness of statement. I am particular in these details, for I believe he deserves this space and criticism, and I think I recognize a new star rising in this western horizon.   F.B.H.

LETTER 26

Christian Register, 10 November 1866

[From our Regular Correspondent.]

CALIFORNIA.

San Francisco, Oct. 9, 1866.

Her Majesty Queen Emma attended Grace Cathedral (Episcopal) on the Sunday after her arrival. One of the dailies, commenting upon the occurrence, says:—"The holy place was *graced* by the presence of Her Majesty Queen Emma," etc., etc. We seldom attempt flunkeyism here; but when we do, as you observe, we excel, as in everything else, and produce something on a par with our gigantic cabbages and potatoes. Yet when the Queen in the afternoon attended St. James,' where there is a boy choir and the service is intoned, another paper alluded to it as "The Church of the Performing Boys," which in a measure restored the equilibrium.

The Bishop of California has been assiduous in his attentions to the Queen, as became the glorious projector of the Hawaiian-Staley-Reformed Catholic Church. The Queen is a member of the Church of England, and it is said not a convert to Staleyism. Apart from these Episcopal courtesies, she has been the recipient of many kindly and hospitable favors from the people and prominent public men here, and if she forgets the *gauche* conduct of the municipal authorities when she first arrived, she will carry away with her next week a pleasant memory of her visit to San Francisco—of attentions that were flattering, yet free from affectation and flunkeyism. She appears to be a modest, well-bred and unassuming lady, and as such will appreciate her reception by the people of California.

During my correspondence with the *Register* I have several times proposed to myself the task of sketching some of the peculiarities of our principal clergymen, who are more remarkable, and exert more influence in this community, than any other class of men. I have thus far refrained from doing so, from a wish to avoid, if possible, those personal details without which I could hardly convey an idea of their influence and labors. In a civilization like ours, where everybody knows everybody else, and neither the habits nor idiosyncrasies of a man are sacred; where there are no cliques or classes, and men are thrown promiscuously together upon one common level and plane of life and experience, the out-of-church, secular influence of a preacher is very important. And as I see by the Eastern papers that the social elegance and piscatorial accomplishments of one clergyman—Dr. Stone—are the subject of complimentary comment by a San Francisco correspondent, I shall justify myself by that precedent. I have, I think, already taken some liberties with our friend, the Rev. Horatio Stebbins. I do not know any better contrast to that bit of New England granite than the stuccoed gentlemen to whom I have referred at the beginning of this letter, and of whom I now purpose to speak more particularly.

William Ingraham Kip, Episcopal Bishop of California, is of fair presence, good family and fair scholastic acquirements. He is the author of one or two semi-ecclesiastical works more remarkable for cultivation and a kind of religious dilettanteism than originality or force. In society he leaves the impression that he mingles with it more for the sake of its forms, distinctions and etiquette, than for its humanity or good will. He is a good deal overcome by the upholstery and furniture of his position. Conservative of things hardly worth preserving, of aristocratic predilections, without possessing the magnanimity and liberality which belong to a self-poised gentleman, vain rather than proud, an European traveller, yet bringing out of that high civilization only its forms and symbols, he is a fair type of a weak nature completely subjugated by the accessories of his position and subordinate to its surroundings. These are hardly the qualities that go to make up a bigot, yet he is the most intolerant of sectarians. It so happens that the highest ministerial talent in the State is among the "dissenters;" they attract the largest audiences; they achieve the greatest success; the most popular and best beloved clergyman on the coast was he whom the bishop did not recognize as being even a Christian—Thomas Starr King—whom he stigmatized as "simply an agitator." Small spite, jealousy and wounded vanity often go as far to make bigots as honest convictions; the intolerance of other ministers may be stronger than intolerance of creed. So intense has been this feeling that in his intercourse with the clergy of the coast he has not only exhibited a want of Christian kindliness, but an absolute lack of ordinary politeness.

He has been so rude and ill-bred as to forfeit even his claims to the standing of a gentleman. He has not the affection of even his adherents. In the church he is unpopular. His sermons are not above the dead level of Episcopal pulpit utterance here, where the church is, with a few exceptions, recruited from mediocrity. He is the "patron" of one or two Episcopal schools, but beyond this his principles do not permit him to be connected with any public movement. He has no politics, hardly any nationality, although his son—a West Point graduate—has served with distinction during the war. At the worst, his is an unfortunate case of dislocation. Transplanted to a kindlier soil, and a less progressive community, these causes which now irritate and bring out his weaknesses would be removed. He would make a capital incumbent of some West End, London church, or rector in some inland town, casting a conscientious Tory vote, and lending the weight of his influence against reform.

The Episcopal church is, *par excellence,* the fashionable church of San Francisco; its audiences are select rather than numerous. Its beautiful ritual, its fine music, its well-appointed accessories hold many cultivated people through their æsthetic inclinations, and atone for the want of force or instruction in the sermon; it reminds others of home and home associations, of older civilizations, of more genial and less material communities, and is dear to them for that alone; its rigid neutrality in politics, its complete isolation from the active works of humanity and progress, make it particularly acceptable to superfine selfishness and ease—it is such a relief to have the church extend a protection to us from the too-irritating calls of duty, that pursue us relentlessly through the week. The Macedonian cry to Paul does not penetrate its cloistered calm and sculptured quiet. We listen to the deep-toned organ, we repeat the supplications made ready for our hand, we abase ourselves becomingly at the proper moments, and we recline in our cushioned-seats and go to sleep comfortably during the sermon, conscious that no heresy is uttered, no irritating doubt suggested, nor any theory promulgated that shall set this jaded brain again into restless activity. What matters it who is bishop or pastor? The church needs not the aid of man—it runs itself. I have no doubt that the bishop understands his duties better than I. Yet I could have wished that Bishop Potter had not died so soon; that he could have brought an influence and power into all this form and ceremonial. The Episcopate could be better filled from among the present clergy.

I have one in my mind who would dignify and make venerable the office—who, if report be correct, should have long ago been inducted into that chair. I refer to Dr. Vermehr, one of the oldest and earliest Episcopal missionaries on the coast. A Hollander of indubitable ancestry, he outranks even the "Kips of Kips Bay," while his culture, continental experience and education are far superior. Gentle, courtly and learned—a bibliophilist, and the best Hebrew scholar in the state —his erudition would have graced, and his years and manners dignified the position. The conservatism, both of age and bookish habits, ought to have lulled the fears of the most timid. As a preacher, his abstract style of thought and slightly foreign accent did not tend to make him popular with the multitude, while his other qualities did not especially commend him to the favor of the bishop. Most unfairly he was retired; after some years of hard missionary labors in building up a church, it was taken away from him, and he was forced to earn his subsistence by school-teaching. He now lives in the country—where he has a vineyard—and the bishop reigns in his stead.

With an exception, our other prominent clergymen are later arrivals—mostly within the past five years. I should like to say something about the advent of new preachers, of the expectations raised from the peculiar style of their annunciation, in a few reflections that belong to the subject; but I find I have already appropriated my space in your columns. I shall take up the subject in another letter. H.

LETTER 27

Christian Register, 1 December 1866

[From our Regular Correspondent.]

CALIFORNIA.

San Francisco, Oct. 30, 1866.

We have been spared the cholera, but we have had Mr. Earle badly. The advent of this Evangelical Revivalist, a few weeks ago, demonstrated the fact that those nervous diseases so prevalent in California may assume, under proper conditions, an epidemic character. Thus far the complaint—like all epidemics—has been confined to the lower orders of society, prevailing more extensively among those whose spiritual systems have been reduced by thin spiritual diet and insufficient mental clothing. Those benighted souls that dwell in the crowded tenement houses of orthodoxy without light or ventilation, are, it is said particularly susceptible. The disease is by no means fatal, is of brief duration, followed often by natural reaction, or, as it is termed, "backsliding," and yields to radical treatment as laid down by Dr. Stebbins in his lecture on "Revivals."

But seriously, if San Francisco be not thoroughly purged of unrighteousness, it will be no fault of Rev. Mr. Earle, who has been expressly imported from the East for that purpose. If in three weeks from date it is not completely evangelized, revived and regenerated, so much the worse for San Francisco; for at about that time Mr. Earle's other engagements oblige him to leave this coast, and Egyptian darkness, unrelieved by revival sunshine or any "gaslight of grace," will descend upon the land. This dismal future is plainly and distinctly forecast by Mr. Earle, in dwelling upon the necessity of immediate conversion. "I must return soon, my time is precious. . . . take advantage of this top wave of revival to get ashore. . . . now is the appointed time," are a few of the arguments by which he prefaces his exhortation. This suggestion that the salvation of two shores of the American continent rests upon him, is not without effect. The coy Christian hesitates no longer. The most premature and incoherent avowal of conversion is preferable to delay and utter damnation. The chaotic, half-baked and underdone character of many of this gentleman's converts may be thus explained.

What there is in this ignorant man to fit him as a apostle of religion on this coast, I utterly fail to discover. Our civilization is insulted by the sending of such a man. He lacks even the magnetic power of his craft. He continually degrades, by indecent figure and symbol, the higher attributes of God. His exhortations are made of anecdotes, many of them the cheapest second-hand illustrations. His arguments, when they are not simple recitations of his former spiritual prowess, are more worthy of the nursery than the pulpit. His language is a violation of every principle of rhetoric, often of grammar. He works upon the fears of his auditors, rather than their affections; his most efficacious illustrations are death-bed scenes and agonies; he exhibits a singular relish in describing mental and physical anguish. When he attempts the sublime he is grotesque, when he tries the humorous, (of which he has no conception) he blasphemes, when he would be affectionate he is maudlin. And this is the man whom a concourse of Orthodox clergyman have called to this coast in the name of the winning, tender, and all-perfect Master.

And yet it would be foolish to deny to him a certain influence and power. Your first impression that he is simply the effect of a certain morbid and abnormal state of religious excitement, a part of the phenomena itself, but unable to explain or control it, would be apt to be wrong. He is shrewd and experienced. He understands what he professes, "the getting up of revivals." He arranges with consummate skill the opening of his meetings; knows how to reject, under the pretence of a second meeting, the large skeptical element which is drawn by curiosity to hear him. He has his few "stool pigeons" (I cannot *without* irreverence give any *other* term to them) planted here and there among his audience; he knows how to segregate the nervous and sanguine temperaments from the lymphatic. He understands the pathology of the complaint better than any other man. His boldness and audacity occasionally reach the sublime. What other man, in the nineteenth century, would dare to address an assemblage of reasoning beings in the following words:—"You who would not do an unkindness or injury to Jesus will please signify it by rising?" What an appeal to the gallantry and good nature of a San Francisco audience. Imagine, if you can, the swaying, elbow-nudging, smirking, giggling mass, rising to their feet, and fancy what must be the proud satisfaction of those Orthodox clergymen who are responsible for the advent of this sensational preacher in San Francisco. And these snap judgments, this injurious way of taking the "sense of the house," is part of the glory of brother Earle and testimony to the efficacy of revivals. Take another instance:—The text is announced,—"Prepare to meet thy God!" Mr. Earle informs the congregation that he will prepare to answer a series of questions, which would naturally be propounded to him by his hearers, on his announcing such a text. The first and most *natural* question, says Mr. Earle, is "Can I not *avoid* meeting my God?" Of course demolishing answers to this most ridiculous question—the last probably that would be conceived by any in the assemblage—are ready. And so on to number two and three, *usque ad nauseam*. Or take his illustrations. Jesus in the text is likened by Mr. Earle to a citizen in Boston who sends a message by him (Mr. E.,) to his son in San Francisco. "Would you say I don't want no message?" anxiously queries this apostle, his voice rising shrilly to a climax. Let us hope that very few of the audience were ungrammatical enough, whatever might be their religious and filial sentiments, to make that reply. Of course the question being put to vote, the "noes" have it, and the religious as well as the filial respectability of that audience is a settled thing.

Much of this is amusing to the disinterested and easy-going spectator, but there is also much that is painful to reverent and refined natures. At these prayer meetings sacred names are bandied about with the recklessness of blasphemy; sacred subjects degraded, and interjections and exclamations abound and offend you like oaths. I have heard it gravely stated by Mr. Earle that "God kept a private secretary hard at work recording Christian conversations." I have heard a young extorter keep up an interjectional play on a certain sacred name, that would have caused his arrest outside of those walls for profanity. I have heard some Christian experiences related that would hardly justify Mr. Earle's statement that "Angels stopped to listen to them, and that all that Christians did in Heaven was to relate them." I remember one man who said that he was "taken badly with religion in the mountains." He did not know how to be converted; but one night he ran out of the house, naked, and hid himself in the woods. His friends brought him back and he "found Jesus!" At this point he became somewhat vague, rambling and incoherent, but finally wound up by warning his brother Christians against *"drinking whiskey!"*

Crowds attend the evening meetings of Mr. Earle, but the conversions are really smaller than would appear and the effect is confined to a very narrow circle. Children and women are his most easy converts, —the paper says "over one hundred young children signified their intention of finding Jesus." I give him two weeks longer—he says three —before the reaction shall begin. I do not look forward to it with pleasure. Mr. Earle has done much to put back civilization and religion in this coast at least twenty years, and if we are flooded by any reacting wave of skepticism or materialism, the few Orthodox clergymen who invited him here are responsible. Messrs. Stone and Scudder, who have been particularly active in this movement, will probably be the first to taste of its bitter fruits, and declaim against the irreligious character of the community.   H.

L E T T E R   2 8

Springfield Republican, 30 March 1867
Springfield Weekly Republican, 6 April 1867

FROM CALIFORNIA.

The Rainy Season—The War Upon the Celestials—The Chinese Fast
Deposing the Irish.

[From Our Special Correspondent.]

San Francisco, February 28, 1867.

It is the rainy season—the "mild, open winter" of the opulent Californian fancy, and the one "incomparable season" of incorrigible California conceit. A preposterous dampness possesses the length and
breadth of the land; there is a sub-aqueous flavor to all things earthly,
and nature drips. Along the skirts of the foot-hills there are strong suggestions of a very recent Silurian beach, and we wouldn't be surprised
at picking up trilobites, brachipods and other damp, uncomfortable
creatures of an early geological period in the roadside puddles, for
the country is in fact but half reclaimed from primal chaos. An area
two-thirds as large as the state of Massachusetts is under water. Snow
lies thick on the Sierras, melting where it laps into the valleys, and
inciting the mountain streams to turbulence and riot. The insurrec-
tionary waters of the Sacramento and American again threaten the
levees of the capital. The farmers are weather-bound in the cities and
can't get home, or are beleaguered in their ranches by the common
enemy. The arcadian hamlets of Poker Flat and Jackass Gulch are
snowed up and most of the portable property has already changed
hands several times through the agency of seven-up or bluff, where-
with these gentle villagers amuse themselves during the winter. In this
remarkable country we seem to exist by comparison and depreciation
of the universe outside of the Pacific coast. The first question asked
a stranger is not, as incorrectly stated, "How do you like California?"
but "Isn't this superior to so-and-so?" Of course the object of all this—

to promote immigration—is laudable, but it is somewhat clumsily executed. It is, at best, advertising and no country, I believe, was ever yet populated by that means. The great emigration movements are grand results, acting from more deeply-seated forces, and are not to be set in motion by a puff.

But one can forgive the press this local weakness for the manly stand which it took in regard to the late riots and outrages on the Chinese. I cannot remember a more unanimous and decided expression of public opinion. With hardly an exception the journals uttered their indignant and unqualified disapprobation of the spirit as well as the manner of this attack upon the inoffensive celestials. That this expression came somewhat late, and that any other would have been ruinous to the state is true, but as acknowledgment of error and broad political views have been rare in California journalism, I am inclined to give them the largest praise for their action. Probably there will not be another riot, but if the public authorities had been more prompt and the best public sentiment more quickly voiced there need not have been any. The attack on these defenseless Chinamen was only the natural climax of a system of tyranny and oppression to which they had been subjected at the hands of the ignorant since their first immigration. Even legislation only tolerated them, and while they were busy in developing the resources of the state, taxed them roundly for the gracious privilege. Regularly every year they were driven out of the mining camps, except when the enlightened Caucasian found it more convenient to rob them—a proceeding which the old statutes in regard to the inadmissibility of their evidence in the courts rendered quite as safe and honorable. They furnished innocent amusement to the honest miner, when gambling, horse-racing, or debauchery palled on his civilized taste, and their Chinese tails, particularly when tied together, cut off or pulled out, were more enjoyable than the Arabian nights' entertainments. Nature seemed to have furnished them with that peculiar appendage for the benefit of the Anglo-Saxon.

In the cities, our California juveniles, who are generally fine young animals, but whose future I watch with some anxiety, made these triangular-eyed foreigners their butt. To throw stones at a Chinaman was an youthful pastime of great popularity, and was to a certain extent recognized and encouraged by parents and guardians, as long as the stones went to their mark with accuracy, and did not come in contact with a superior civilization. It may be readily imagined how this supercilious ignoring of their rights by the Americans and better class of European residents, encouraged and fostered the blind hatred and active malice of our Celtic citizens, who from the first regarded them with a jealousy and malevolence only equal to their old intolerance of the negro. Convinced from the beginning of the superiority of freckles, red hair and a brick-dusty epidermis, over the smooth, shining, India-ink-washed faces of their Chinese rivals, they at once put the Mongolians on the level of the African, and abused them on theological grounds. It was only when they attempted to settle the question of average brain capacity, by breaking the Chinese head to more conveniently examine its contents, that they were checked. As I have before suggested they have spoiled even their chances of getting legislation in their favor or making political capital of what they term their wrongs. They had a meeting the other night, but the few stale political hacks who were their orators, and the old conservative twaddle about "white races," "puritanism," "nigger quality," gave the whole affair, for them, a most luckless and unpopular aspect.

In regard to the facts upon which most of the arguments in favor of restricting Chinese labor and immigration are based, there is no doubt that the Chinese are gradually deposing the Irish from their old, recognized positions in the ranks of labor. The Chinese not only fill their places, but fill them more acceptably. As servants they are quick-witted, patient, obedient and faithful, and the old prerogatives of Bridget and Norah in the domestic circle are seriously threatened by the advent of these quiet, clean and orderly male chambermaids and cooks. That John Chinaman will eventually supplant Bridget and Patrick in menial occupations seems to be a settled fact. I see nothing for Bridget and Patrick to do except to progress, and to remember that they have long enjoyed a monopoly in their peculiar avocations, often to the exclusion of native Americans. But it was my intention to simply state facts and waive any argument based thereon.

Of John Chinaman's religious and moral influence on society we know but little. He is certainly a pagan. He prays to the devil and buys his wife, two things that are of course inconsistent with our high civilization, where the devil is never propitiated and all matrimonial engagements are based on pure affection. He has an absurd system of moral philosophy of his own, which dates back many centuries. But his idolatries are secret, his vices are not obtrusive, and his dissipations, like opium smoking, affect no one but himself. Generally he is abstemious; nature has gotten him up economically, with a view to a crowded population, and he asks very little of her in return. In disposition he is amiable and patient, civil and decorous, and does not even seem to know that he is an exciting "problem" in our civilization, much less to be inclined to take advantage of the fact. His usual deportment is characterized by a certain deprecatory air, as if he knew that there was a great deal too many of him, and was sorry for it.   F.B.H.

———————

LETTER 29

Springfield Republican, 14 May 1867
Springfield Weekly Republican, 18 May 1867

FROM SAN FRANCISCO.

———————

The China Steamship Line—The Japanese Commissioners—Interesting Breach of Promise Case—The Russian American Treaty—Relief for the South.

[From Our Special Correspondent.]

San Francisco, April 10, 1867.

Since my last the Colorado, which left here on the lst of January to open steam communication with China and Japan, has returned and has started on her second trip. Being somewhat behind her schedule time, she had barely discharged her freight and passengers before her prow was again pointed westward, and she was once more speeding on that voyage, which even under steam and the most favorable circumstance is tedious, dreary and monotonous. I did not envy her officers their six months' experience, made up of so much sea and so little shore. The China mail line is hardly adapted to pleasure trips. Even the so-called Pacific is turbulent at times, and lively cyclones waltz up and down the China coast. For the first thousand miles out of San Francisco there are sporadic intervals of awful monotony—vast gaps of dullness and protracted periods of vacuity, when the grasshopper is a burden and desire fails and the passengers stare blankly at the blank expanse of waters. It is at such times that, on all sea-voyages, amateur concerts, amateur readings, amateur newspapers and amateur celebrations and speeches are conceived from those depths of imbecility which the human mind only achieves when it goes seriously at work to amuse itself. There is something indescribably affecting in those ghastly preparations for cheerfulness and the deliberate declarations of an intention to be funny. "The world," says somebody, "would be bearable if it were not for its amusements." It is only when people are weak enough to preserve memorials of these occasions—say a paper published on board a steamer, or a speech delivered under the same circumstances, that we get any adequate conception of the subterfuges to which the human intellect descends to avert insanity. These are the puny weapons with which the steamer traveler opposes what M. Hugo would call the ananke of space, of silence and of eternity typified by the illimitable ocean. A voyage to China is a voyage from New York to San Francisco doubled, with the Isthmus and female companionship subtracted. But it is whispered that there were more material discomforts on the return trip from China. The table was poorly provided, and it is alleged that the nutritious but homely bean formed a prominent feature of the bill of fare. Whether this vegetable was introduced by way of preparing the passengers for the popular Californian dish, or whether it was from a mere ignoble economy on the part of the company's agent in China, is not known. A free and independent press have preserved ominous silence on the subject.

The Colorado brought the Japanese commissioners, who, after a brief stay in this city left in the last Panama steamer for Washington. In the few days that they were here, they exhausted all the wonders of San Francisco, and I shudder to think, must have been bored fearfully. They visited the forts, federal and municipal offices, factories and refineries, the mint and the asylums. They were haled out of their beds by daylight in the morning and bundled into carriages, where, painfully conspicuous by reason of their swords and umbrellas, they were driven frantically hither and thither, and asked to be astonished. They were waylaid at every step by conceited Californians, who demanded their compliments with the air of a footpad. School children sang for them with that breezy shrillness which is peculiar to a generation growing up under the influence of our summer winds. But all these and other courtesies and attentions our Japanese diplomats received with a stolid gravity and undemonstrative tranquility, which was particularly trying to the vanity of their hosts. They were invariably accompanied by a servant who carried a small black leather valise, which looked as though it might have contained a change of linen for the commissioners, but which actually held the veritable letter of the tycoon to the president. This sacred document being considered as a kind of protecting ægis may have accounted for their phlegm. The fact, too, that they also carried two swords and could at any time, when the attentions of their entertainers became insupportable, have calmly performed the "hari-kari," and so put themselves out of their misery, doubtless had its tranquilizing effect. For a Japanese envoy to coolly rip up his bowels during a very long-winded and formal address, would no doubt be considered by them as an extremely delicate piece of diplomacy, and in fact rather commends itself to my western sense of fitness. This idea of the happy dispatch is apt, very naturally, to affect you in your intercourse with a Japanese nobleman. You are nervously cautious of giving offense, holding as you do the integrity of his diaphragm in your safe keeping. Your eye anxiously wanders to that usually unattractive part of his person, and you feel relieved when he at last parts from you with his digestive apparatus unimpaired. I can't say that conversation with such impending abdominal possibilities is either easy or natural. You are apt to accede to your visitor's propositions with a feverish alacrity. You recognize a symbolic ventriloquism in his speech which renders easy conversation out of the question. He talks to you from a belly as unsafe and uncertain as the "vexed bowels" of Mr Tupper. I am told that the etiquette of the "happy dispatch" requires actual excision and protrusion. Thus, in the Japanese tragedy of "The Damio's Revenge or the Maid of Hokadadi," when the faithful attendant rushes in upon the heroine with the dreadful news, she asks with broken accents and national periphrasis, "He—then—di-gests—no-longer?" the messenger replies, with noble directness, "Madam, I have seen his bowels!" The usual newspaper form is not, "He put a period to his existence," but simply, "He divided his colon."

The present commissioners are very intelligent, and are much superior to the doubtful embassy that visited Buchanan some years ago, and turned the heads of fair New York. They are of higher rank, a prince and governor being among them. They seem to be well educated, understanding the theory and principles of many things which they saw practically demonstrated for the first time. The secretary of

the commission is a Japanese author of some popularity, and has translated a history of the United States, the constitution, and Declaration
of Independence, into his own tongue, with comments and annota-
tions. He has also written a treatise on European civilization, besides
occasionally translating from English and American papers, accounts
of discoveries, inventions, and scientific data. The commissioners are
obliged by virtue of their office to transmit an account or daily journal
of their experience, and I presume that a very detailed and accurate
description of our Pacific civilization will, by the time this reaches you,
be in the possession of the Japanese state department. Their literature
is marked by a refreshing simplicity and good faith. The secretary
translated one of Dr Ayer's advertising almanacs, even to the marginal
facetiæ, and transmitted a copy to Japan, as a work of a national and
benevolent character. All this of course has no relation to the specific
object of the commission, which, when it transpires, will create some
little excitement in Washington. As it was told to me as a secret, I am
of course burning to get rid of it. Nothing but a perhaps too sensitive
regard for the bowels of my friend, the secretary, restrains my pen at
this moment.

Scandal which acquires an intensity and keenness of relish in this
community, where everybody knows everybody else, and reputations
like fortunes are recent, has held its Saturnalia over the details of the
great breach of promise case of Clark *vs* Reese. Michael Reese, the
defendant, is a San Francisco millionaire, whose parsimony and mean-
ness is even remarkable for San Francisco, whose rich men are not
generally liberal, public spirited, philanthropic or benevolent. Reese
is, however, a miser, and does not spend money on himself or for his
own pleasures, a fact which debars him from even the sympathies of
his fellow capitalists. At first it seemed absurd to identify his nature
with the generous and subduing passion claimed by the plaintiff to
have animated his actions, but when the trial developed the manner
of his alleged courtship, the explanation was given; $1.25 for a pair of
gloves, gingerbread (substituted for sponge cake as less indigestible),
a gold buckle, valued at $2.50, in fact a total expenditure of about
$10 made up the golden shower in which this financial Jove visited
this Danae. The defense set up a denial of the promise and alleged
improper conduct on the part of the plaintiff. Suborned witnesses and
the most palpable perjury disgraced the trial, with occasional reve-
lations of a character unfit for publication. The verdict of the jury
was flattering to neither plaintiff nor defendant. Five thousand dollars

was given to repair those wounded feelings for which the fair plaintiff asked $100,000. It is well known that if her character had been above suspicion she would have recovered the whole amount, while if the defendant had been a more liberal man she would have got nothing. It was an eminently Californian verdict. Another case against another wealthy Californian is on the calendar and the anticipated exposures are already spoken of with a perceptible smacking of the lips and epicurean enthusiasm.

The confirmation of the Russian American treaty is received with extreme satisfaction by all who know the real value of the territory ceded, and they comprise every intelligent inhabitant of the Pacific coast. You can hardly conceive of the importance of this northern purchase to us. We know the value of the fisheries, the furs, the probable mineral development, and could not understand the hesitation of Congress to ratify the treaty.

The southern relief committee are doing well. They sent yesterday $30,000 and expect to send more. This may not seem much to the state that contributed so munificently to the sanitary commission, but Thomas Starr King is dead, and with that rare apostle, who infused into this hard money-loving community something of his own tenderness and magnanimity, and who cheated the people into the belief that they were generous when they were only appreciative, lies buried the secret of his success.   F.B.H.

LETTER 30

Christian Register, 18 May 1867

[From our Regular Correspondent.]

CALIFORNIA.

San Francisco, April 15, 1867.

Since the Sanitary and Christian Commissions we have had no popular benevolent enterprise as successful as that of the Southern Relief Committee. Organized only two weeks ago, they have collected $50,000 in this city alone, and expect to increase the amount to $100,000. Taking everything into consideration the gift is really more creditable to California than the larger she showered upon the Sanitary Commission. It is the result of conscientious and deliberate convictions of duty on the part of the givers. There have been no enthusiastic outbursts of feeling—no Californian emulation and "out-bidding." No Thomas Starr King has risen to kindle audiences with patriotic fire or thrill their hearts with persuasive eloquence. On the contrary, while most of the old Sanitary Committee are connected with this organization, too many of its exponents and prompters are well-known Southern sympathizers and disloyalists—men who during the rebellion were recognized as openly hostile to the government, who never aided in the benevolent organizations of the war, and who now ask aid with the air of demanding damages. That these men have not prejudiced the merits of their cause in the estimation of the benevolent is an evidence of the true charity of this gift, and would be an honor to a less impulsive people than Californians. Our prominent Union men have, I think, made a mistake in not forcing themselves to the front in this matter and so gaining the confidence of the loyal masses. It never should have acquired its present sectional position. There was a preponderance of old peace democrats and tender-footed Union men among the signatures of the first "Call" for a public meeting. The Rev. Mr. Fitzgerald of the Methodist Church South,—so violent a rebel that he was under *surveillance* of the Military Commander of this district, early in the war, and Bishop Kip, whose snobbish deference to a few wealthy and aristocratic secessionists placed the Episcopal Church in California in a disloyal attitude all through the war, were certainly new names to see upon any call for a public meeting that was to deal with any subject of vital importance to the country. The meeting, at which the governor presided, was addressed by Fitzgerald, Stone and Cohn, clergymen. Rev. Mr. Stebbins was down for a speech, but was unfortunately absent. Liberal Christianity was nevertheless represented by a lay member, R. B. Swain, Esq., in a brief and concise address. The meeting, however, did not warm the people up to any enthusiasm. As I said before, they gave in grim silence, and sympathized with their Southern brethren with set teeth and one hand on their revolvers.

But while San Francisco gave $50,000 in pure charity, she spent nearly the same amount in a prize fight. Forty thousand dollars was the sum estimated to have been collected in tickets, fares, admission fees and other expenses to the grounds at San Mateo, where "the great fight between Tommy Chandler and Doony Harris" was to have come off. A large amphitheatre of benches, capable of seating 3000 people, had been erected—matters of this kind being arranged in California with the old Roman audacity of conception. Many solid, respectable, and church-going citizens were present. Although the object of the gathering was well known, in deference to existing legal objections the affair was called a "picnic," and so printed on the tickets. It was a bit of exquisite irony. Here, only seventeen miles from San Francisco, in "a green cuplike hollow of the downs," in a virgin April meadow, as yet too fresh and undefiled for any feet save those of innocent children in some holiday festival, five thousand men assembled to take part in an eminently bucolic festival, whose chief sport was the pounding of two brutes by each other. They looked around at the smiling spring landscape, and jocularly speculated on how much of it would be visible to the battered eyes of the bruisers after the fight was over. Here they came, but here they were disappointed. For lo, a quiet little man suddenly appeared in the ring between the two combatants and their seconds. Unarmed and untraincd, without backers, bottle-holders or seconds, this third champion threw down his glove of defiance in the ring in the shape of a warrant. Alack! no training on raw beefsteaks, no pounding of sand-bags, no sweatings, no runnings or rubbings had prepared them to successfully resist this puny individual whose name was Law and whose sporting title was the "Sheriff of San Mateo County." A crowd of brutal and incensed men—savage as beasts about to be deprived of an expected meal—pressed around him with oaths and threats. For nearly half an hour his life was in constant peril. He was hustled and shoved about, but his purpose was immovable. He had come to prevent the fight, and he eventually succeeded. The highly developed men of Might gave way to the representative of Right. His success was attributable mainly to a singular fact, which it is difficult for any but a Californian to properly appreciate, and to note which is my excuse for troubling your readers with this unpleasant episode. The greater portion of the mob recognized the fact that the sheriff was doing his duty, and in accordance with the law, I am told, and from what I know of these singular people, sincerely believe that if any violence had been offered that officer in the performance of his duty, or if any attempt had been made to openly disobey him, the very men who were clamorous for the fight to go on would have rushed to sustain him. This is one of the strange paradoxes of California civilization. The same men who will break the law through very wantonness, will defend it through principle. I would trust any great question involving radical right and justice quite as securely with these people as with an older and more cautious civilization. Meanwhile, if any reader of the *Register* wishes to know the sequel of this picnic he may learn that the parties had their "debate" elsewhere, and proved doubtless to the satisfaction of all concerned which was the greatest and more enduring animal. Perhaps California may yet send the victor to Congress —the Great West's set-off to Morrissey.

Our winter has been unusually prolonged and severe—although I believe that is the common yearly meteorological commentary. An April shower of great violence, lasting some two or three days, brought up the rivers to their maximum overflow, and a violent gale at the same time caused great loss of life and property along the coast. In the mountains the snow has been almost continuous. You have an idea that snow of ten and fifteen feet in depth represents a pretty severe winter blockade. Why, our Pacific Railroad goes through snow thirty and forty feet deep. The smoke of the locomotive as you approach the summit of the Sierras, rises between snow banks sometimes one hundred feet above the track. Looking back on the foot-hills the road seems to pass through a canal of white marble whose walls vary from fifteen to twenty feet in height. When you leave the cars on the summit, you walk or ride by submerged telegraph poles, that stick sometimes two or three feet above the snow—more often trailing its wires along their surface. Think of cabins entirely hidden, with their chimneys melting a small crater around their tops as they smoke on the roadside. In some places the only evidence of habitation is a deep incline cut through the snow, marking the ingress to some buried farmhouse. A few of the settlers build their houses on props raising them up as the snow falls. Of course there will be an uncomfortable revelation in the summer when the snow melts, and real estate falls. You will say you have read something like this in Munchausen, but these are facts. Imagine what ought to be the fiction of such a people.   H.

LETTER 31

Springfield Republican, 6 June 1867
Springfield Weekly Republican, 8 June 1867

FROM CALIFORNIA.

A Mexican Jubilation—Reminiscences of Telegraph Hill—Butchertown and Swinesville—Arrival of Senator Conness—Departure for Our Russian Possessions—The Southern Relief Fund.

[From our Special Correspondent.]

San Francisco, May, 1867.

My windows are rattling from a salute now being fired on yonder hill. The gentlemen who are thus disturbing the peaceful close of a calm spring day are our friends, the liberal Mexicans of San Francisco, and the occasion is the anniversary of some victory, I think that of Puebla, in 1862. The firing is energetic, and the guns are heavily charged; if the percussion of blank cartridges could drive the French out of Mexico, I tremble for the fate of Maximilian. But here we are accustomed to these windy pronunciamentos, and their potency is somewhat modified by the fact that both parties, imperialists and liberals, use the same locality for the same purpose. The quantity of powder burnt in this harmless rivalry is considerable, and a certain degree of insecurity attaches to the glass windows in the neighborhood. But by a wise adjustment of natural laws there are few costly windows about here, Telegraph Hill and vicinity having long lost their fashionable and aristocratic inhabitants, and being given up to native Californians, foreigners and the playful and aboriginal goat. Howbeit, the Mexican flag waves proudly from the old signal station, and the men, boys and goats are having a good time. It is nearly twenty years since that same flag rightfully flew from that summit, where now a few tumble down shanties and a score of men and boys are all that represent the old possessors of the soil. I trust there is nothing ominous in the coincidence, but of late years the Eagle and the Serpent have been unfortunate.

Perhaps the emblem is unlucky and suggests too much internecine clawing and biting.

This northern portion of San Francisco still retains some of the characteristics of the early days, and is still affected by the native Californian, and even by some of the American pioneers. From Telegraph Hill the old Californians watched the American whalers rounding the point and later the American war ships; from this summit the emigrants of '49 anxiously looked for the slow steamers, in those dreary homesick days, when letters were two months coming from "the states," and men, whose bones lie in Lone Mountain cemetery, came to "stay for a year." This slope was the nucleus and germ of the present metropolis; the root of that tree, whose branches are now pushing southerly and westwardly toward the ocean. In rambling over the slopes you occasionally come across a veritable adobe dwelling—one, an old landmark, was lately taken down to make way for the slow improvement of this locality. Here are weather-beaten, roughly-boarded, unpainted cottages, with lace curtains at the windows, and the open door permitting a glimpse of an elegantly furnished room, a lace-draped couch and the black-eyed, black-shawled and white-skirted inmates. Or you may chance to meet a dark-skinned man, whose glazed hat with its preternatural breadth of brim, and red sash, is a reminiscence of those better days when all hats were broad-brimmed, and everybody, from the governor down, wore sashes, and a limpsiness and laxity pervaded male and female attire, very different from the precision, starchiness and rigidity introduced by *los Americanos.* The women then never wore corsets; the men never wore braces. Buttons and hooks and eyes are as surely a sign of superior civilization and refinement as strings, sashes, bandages and wrappings are evidences of barbarism. Why doesn't some Teufelsdrock in a new Sartor Resartus classify mankind according to the types indicated by dress, or show man's progress through the successive stages of "enwrapping," "bandaging," "tying," until we come to the perfection of "lacing" and "buttoning." Or, taking Buckle's theory of the youth, manhood and old age of nations, why not illustrate with the many wrappings of the *pupa* stage of civilization, the close-fitting garments of maturity and manhood, and the return to the dressing gown and "lean and slippered pantaloon" of senility and decay. But I fear that I am getting out of my depth, and that all this is inconsequent to the matter in hand

and out of place in this breezy, matter of fact atmosphere. The climate is fatal to abstract speculation.

To get back to our sheep, which are goats here, the city has grown away from this infelix locality, and left it in the "rearward of fashion," with its Chinese quarters and "Barbary coast"—as the back slums of Pacific street are called—both of which are on the skirts of the historic hill already mentioned. Obeying some blind, mysterious instinct, the city has moved southerly and westwardly, although hills have had to be leveled and waters bridged for that purpose. When three years ago the Mission bay flowed uninterruptedly between the South Beach and the Potrero, now a city railroad carries passengers over the Long Bridge in an air line to that point which was of old reached by the slower process of following the curved trend of the shore. Butchertown and Swinesville—the slaughter pen of San Francisco, and long the eye sore of the city—Butchertown and Swinesville, whose "strange, invisible perfume hits the sense of the adjacent wharves," and speedily clears them of loungers; Butchertown and Swinesville, whose peculiar fragrance comprises all the smells which Coleridge catalogued in Cologne, with a certain original local stink as yet unclassified—have been ordered away by the supervisors. Although the butchers fought long and gallantly for delay, their doom is sealed. They are to stand no longer in the way of the march of improvement or the noses of the people. Vine embowered cottages will probably take the place of the old shambles, and the settlement will be cut up into building lots, but for a long time it will doubtless be haunted by the tread of murdered cattle and the squealing of phantom swine.

But to turn from this vulgar form of corruption to the purer field of politics, our "only sober senator," the Hon John Conness, arrived in the last steamer, and a thrill of excitement is lent to the political canvass. In accordance with that affecting custom which is the pride and boast of every American citizen, a brass band, composed equally of office holders and musicians, waited upon the honorable senator the other evening and proceeded to play Yankee Doodle and Hail Columbia beneath his balcony—the accepted significance of which movement was that they should like to know something about the state of the country. After being introduced by the new naval officer, the honorable senator, apparently in reply to the bassoon, took occasion to say that he felt pride in his humble position as their representative, and that the eyes of the nation were generally directed to California with admiration and regard. He remarked also that a great work had just been successfully accomplished. It needed perhaps no senator come from Washington to tell us this, but it no doubt satisfied the bassoon. After having tacitly contradicted the statement of his enemies that he had courted Johnson's favor, by denouncing his policy in the strongest terms, the honorable senator retired. The band then played a popular air to the effect that it was ever of the honorable senator that they were fondly dreaming, that his gentle voice their spirit could charm, that he was the star that beamed o'er their slumbers, &c., &c., and then they too retired. Messrs Higby, Bidwell and McRuer were not serenaded, I believe, at least by that band. Bidwell is one of the candidates for governor and has just informed the Sacramento Union that he has not entered into any political combination with Conness. I really cannot say how many candidates there are for this office; their name is legion, and every day we hear of a new man. San Francisco has three, Pixley, Fay and Gorham, Union. The democrats trot out the usual list of stale, scratched hacks. "Bascom's grocery" at the "Four corners" is liberally represented. There is little choice among the political aspirants; they all have the general qualification of unfitness. But I begin to think that I am getting beyond my depth again. Accept this as a conscientious desire on my part to fulfill my duties as a general chronicler of Pacific news.

We have had a pleasant spring. Let me record, by the way of penitence for my general assaults on this climate, two or three lovely days when the air was balmy and soft, the sunlight golden, the sky a mild cerulean and deliciously shaded here and there with flocculent *cirrostratus*—days when a warm haze overlaid the hard outlines of Sausalito and Tamalpais; when sweet virginal whispers were on the air, and nature seemed coy and timid, and had quite forgotten the bold, brazen way in which she usually showers her favors on Californians. The thermometer ranged no higher than 75 degrees, yet these spoiled and pampered San Franciscoans, who require the bracing gales as they do their bitters, talked of "debilitating heat," and sighed for fog and nor'westers. Certain bold men drew out linen coats and trowsers from their long seclusion at the bottom of steamer trunks, and arrayed themselves for a brief holiday. Straw hats appeared, the never-failing verandahs of our city architecture were for once actually serviceable, and street doors and windows yawned widely under the aperient influences of spring. But presto! the wind changed to the north and blew out a blast that speedily closed the pores of San Francisco.

The Oriflamme leaves here on the 1st of June for our new Russian possessions. She will take out a large number of practical men, who will be able to tell us the real value, within a few dollars, of our late purchase. I shall let you know the result.

The famine relief fund gathers slowly. The amount realized will be creditable to California, though the contributions have not come in as spontaneously as in the case of the sanitary commission.   F.B.H.

LETTER 32

Springfield Republican, 15 July 1867
Springfield Weekly Republican, 20 July 1867

FROM CALIFORNIA.

The Republican State Convention—Fraud and Trickery—George C. Gorham the Candidate for Governor—The State Printer—A General Riot and Rumpus.

[From Our Special Correspondent.]
San Francisco, June 15, 1867.

Our Union state convention has just finished its labors, and we have been treated to a spectacle of corruption unexampled even in the palmiest days of New York municipal politics. Fraud, trickery and bribery have triumphed; not as adjuncts of better measures, not disguised as principles, but solely by the force of their intrinsic merits as fraud, trickery and bribery. The corrupt means themselves have only been equaled in enormity by the perfect audacity and boldness of their execution.

The primary election which created the San Francisco delegates to the state convention was a preliminary swindle. A corrupt "ring" kept the polls to the exclusion of respectable and well known republicans and admitted "broom rangers" and old time copperheads with a flimsy test oath on the present reconstruction question, so worded as to be an insult to old Union men; while from the absence of any retrospective quality, it gathered all the dregs of the old peace-preaching democratic organization. The Irish vote was captured by an unmeaning "eight hour labor" resolution and an "anti-coolie" platform, the latter being in fact merely a protest to the importation of Chinese slaves instead of the wholesale rigorous prohibition against the race demanded by our amiable Celtic brethren. In brief, the swindle was perfect; the only actual test being corruption, the only real prohibition being honesty. The "ring" elected their delegates; the "People's party"—a municipal organization that sprang from the ashes of the old vigilance committee —was beaten by their old enemies, the "roughs," "boys," and "short hairs," who now comprise the controlling elements of our Union party, and who make up by ultra radicalism and extreme principles, their lack of respectability and legitimacy. It was hard to see old republicans, who stood by the nation when the state trembled on the verge of secession, overborne by these bran-new loyalists, these "eleventh hour" radicals. I know of one voter, an abolitionist when abolitionism was considered disgraceful, the publisher of a free soil paper at a time and in a community that was perilous to the life of the publisher, whose vote was challenged by one of the men, who, five years before, had persecuted him in the interests of pro-slavery. It was not strange that a large number of Union men preferred to stay at home during the primary election than be submitted to such impertinence, or that such a resolution was exactly what the "ring" looked for and calculated upon.

The prime mover of this corrupt organization, the chief of this unholy junto, the man who enjoys the distinction of being the "smartest" politician of the state, the leader whose lion's share of the spoils is the nomination for governor, which he has just secured, is George C. Gorham. If history be silent regarding his services or qualities, or if the eastern reader does not readily recognize his name among the great West's favored sons, it is because his successes have been chiefly in the world of minor politics, and his walk the back stairs of public office. He was private secretary to Governor Low, until a more profitable office was made for him by his friends, Justice Field and Senator Conness, who combined the United States district and circuit clerkships in one, and ousted the district Judge's appointee for their favorite. As the governor's private secretary, he gave his influence to the lobby, of which he soon became the head. His gubernatorial aspirations were at first received with a smile. Bidwell, a rich land holder in the interior, and Frank Pixley, a talented San Francisco lawyer, were the more favorite candidates for nomination, and even the more cunning politicians looked upon Gorham's pretentions as a blind. Rash and too-confident electors! That insignificant, scorbutic looking district clerk, of mediocre attainments and abilities, unknown except to politicians, was already master of the situation. It was to him that other nominees must look for support. His lobby experience has already taught him the follies and foibles of mankind, and nature had kindly left out of his own organization that unprofitable weakness which prevents a man from using his fellow man like merchandise. Although an anti-slavery man he had no scruples about trading in the honor or principles of men or of buying and selling their preferences and opinions. The state in fact woke up to find this obscure man the exponent of the Union organization and the head of the state ticket.

In vain had the four most prominent, most independent, and I had almost written most influential journals of the state, namely the Sacramento Union, San Francisco Bulletin, Alta and Call, protested against the iniquity of the convention, and the impudence of Mr Gorham's aspirations. The press for once seemed powerless. The only metropolitan journal that urged his claims was a ridiculous, moss-trooping sheet called The American Flag, conspicuous for its insane bombast, extra-loyalty and extra-venality; an incipient sort of New York Herald, plus its slang and slander, and minus its ability and enterprise. Its services were rewarded by the committee with the gift of the nomination of state printer to its proprietor, Mr McCarthy, a gentleman who had previously been presented to the grand jury for indictment as a libeler of private character. Yet this ridiculously illiterate and notoriously unscrupulous sheet was complimented in the convention by Mr J. W. Dwinelle, a San Francisco lawyer who has some claim to respectability and literary education. This gentleman virtually assured the convention, in a few happy illustrations, that the modest Unionism of a scholar and gentleman was not as respectable as that of an illiterate politician, that an ignorant partisan sheet was better than a cultivated Union journal, and that in short a Bunkum Flagstaff and Independent Echo was superior to an Evening Post. Whereat the convention howled their applause, and elected Mr McCarthy state printer.

You perceive by this that we are progressing, and rapidly approximating that perfection of corruption which distinguishes our older eastern political brethren. The late convention, considered as the offspring of a community only 17 years old, is something to be proud of. Indeed, I think our last legislative lobby could have taught their New York brethren one or two new ideas. Here we are not hampered by any of those conventional disguises which too often obstruct the easy practice of vice in older communities.

There is, however, a movement on foot to decapitate the ticket and throw off the objectionable gubernatorial nominee. The printers also are incensed against McCarthy's nomination as state printer, chiefly, I fear, because he employed "rats" on his paper during its precarious existence, and partly because he is not a professional printer, which they declare the state printer ought to be. But if this revolutionary idea of fitness for office should prevail in this one instance, it would establish such a dangerous precedent for the rest of the ticket that I tremble to speculate upon it any further.   F.B.H.

LETTER 33

Springfield Republican, 11 September 1867
Springfield Weekly Republican, 14 September 1867

FROM CALIFORNIA.

Summer in San Francisco—Vacation Idleness—A Recipe for California Mountain Scenery—Bierstadt's Yo Semite—Natural Antagonism of Natives and Tourists—California Farming—San Jose and its Model Hotel.

[From Our Special Correspondent.]
San Francisco, July 29, 1867.

It was hot weather along the Pacific slope during the early part of July; hot in San Francisco, where the summer winds and fogs pretermitted their regular evening calls, and the mercury one night quietly climbed to 90 degrees and staid there, with half San Francisco sitting up in shirt sleeves, watching it in fearful expectancy; hot everywhere within 70 miles of the coast, where the regular "trades" usually modify the sun's fierceness—everywhere except in the Sierras that have a temperature of their own. For several days the iron-bound, rocky coast of California, from the Heads of the Blessed Trinity to the City of the Angels, glittered and glowed to a red heat in the direct solar rays. It was hot in the Santa Cruz mountains, where the writer of this had gone for his summer vacation, and where the thermometer marked 105 degrees in the shade. The thermal retrospect hardly seems possible to-night, as I listen to the dismal tolling of the fog bell at Alcatraces, and watch the cold, grey cloud enwrapping the hills of San Francisco. But after this slight hint of what the climate can do in the way of orthodox summer, one is apt to recognize a certain blunt sincerity in the rude breeze that buffets a healthy color into the cheek, and a not unpleasant alterative in the fog,—that saline draught which all San Francisco is obliged to swallow daily. The fact that the cholera is striding westward across the plains perhaps makes us less impatient of our surly sanitary guardians.

I might have told the readers of The Republican something about my humble summer retreat, leaving the Big Trees, Yo Semite, Shasta and the Geysers, the heroics of California scenery, for the poetic pens of more enthusiastic correspondents. But, although the theme was suited to my less ambitious style, the weather was not. To lie on one's back under a tree, and outstare the staring, unlidded sky, seemed to be the only appropriate employment. To write anything more important than one's initials on the back of a tree or a faded leaf appeared simply ridiculous. Nature seemed to indicate the receptive attitude as being the only fit condition for the human mind, but alas, poetic contemplation and philosophy were too often a preliminary to vulgar somnolence and snoring. Books of all kinds were sweetly soporific; the leaves of the magazines were of poppy and mandragora. I have consequently but a vague recollection of murmuring water and whispering trees, with unpleasantly lucid intervals of mountain dust heated by the red-hot expletives of teamsters and drivers, of the odors of "fried" beefsteaks mingling with the spicery of pines, of a prevailing and all pervading flavor of horse blanket. The horse is a noble and faithful animal; as an intimate companion, however, he smells vilely. The heroes of mediæval romance, whose proud boast it was to share their bed and board with their faithful chargers, undoubtedly also shared the noble animal's peculiar odor.

If I failed to record my impressions then and there, I doubt if it

were worth while to recall them now. Like the musical springs with
which these mountains abound, the draught must be quaffed at the
fountain; the effervescence can't be bottled and transported. But as
mineral water may be analyzed and made, I can offer a recipe for ordinary California mountain scenery which will give you eastern folk
some faint idea of its integral parts. Take an average eastern mountain range. Add twenty feet to the circumference, and some fifty or
a hundred feet to the hight of the pines. Take some of the largest
of them, strip off the bark and substitute the outer husk of an ex-
ceedingly stringy and fibrous cocoa-nut, dye it a dull red like faded
Russia leather, and you have "the redwood,"—a tree that can hardly
be called beautiful or imposing. Pick out the most graceful birch that
can be found, stain its paper bark a most exquisite rose tint, deepening
toward the bough and branch firicals, give its foliage the wavy smooth-
ness of a japonica leaf; in autumn, hang upon its boughs pendant,
grapelike clusters of scarlet berries, and you have the *madrone*—the
very queen and goddess of the California Alpine forest. Scatter here
and there the buckeye with its spike of odorous summer blossoms, the
"prison oak,"—the only shrub that imitates in its variegated leaf the
autumnal tints of your eastern woodlands,—the *chemisal*, the "fern,"
—so large as to give you some idea of the material from which the
coal beds were formed,—and fill up the interstices with dusty stubble
and you have the summer vegetation. Denude the sides of the mountains some twenty degrees until you have them nearly perpendicular;
deepen your ravines about two hundred feet, let the trees on the opposite sides of the mountain mingle their branches together, and you
have a *canon*. Turn a little water,—a very little will do for a summer
prospect, add logs, roots, fallen trees and bridges, and you have a
creek which shall vary in width from one to one hundred feet, according to the season of the year. Everywhere keep in view the effect of
six months drouth and six months rain, and the attrition and denuda-
tion caused by mountain torrents. Then mingle with the whole a slight
volcanic flavor, shown in thermal springs, bits of scoria, burnt and
blackened rock, and an occasional crater-like indentation in the highest peaks, and you have California coast mountain scenery. Multiply
this by 100 and it gives you the Sierras, plus the snow and minus the
vegetation. This of course does not give you the atmosphere. Neither
does the original. Neither does the stereoscope, which resembles the
media through which all California scenery is viewed more than any-

thing else I can think of. Go and see Bierstadt's wonderful "Domes of the Yo Semite." If what the critics say be true, he has given them an atmosphere so poetic, so delicious, that one does not care to see the original bleak, bare, coldly outlined and sharply incisive monoliths in their original, practical conditions. That atmosphere, those clouds, that charming tinting exists not in the valley; neither did it exist in the original sketches in that clever artist's own portfolio, as I once had the pleasure of seeing them. Is it the haze which distance and a poetic memory lends to the past, or must we thank thee, O A.B., for granting us through that larger sense of consistency and harmony which belongs to art, the charm which nature has so churlishly denied us?

There is, however, a natural antagonism between the resident native and the poetic tourist or correspondent. It is not pleasant to have people around you falling into spasms of admiration and enthusiasm after an hour's acquaintance with things which you think you have thoroughly comprehended, and which you admire—if at all—with a judicious calmness. When your tourist talks of the impassiveness, ignorance or want of enthusiasm of the native, as is his fashion, receive his statement with extreme caution. I confess my sympathies are greatly with the natives and inhabitants of be-praised and be-toured localities. I am inclined to think there is some good reason for the half-superciliousness and ill-disguised scorn which characterize most guides. May not the predatory and grasping character of most of the cicerones at famous places be traced back to a more noble spirit of resistance to this poetic tyranny? What right has your dapper man of fancy, traveler or poet, to impose upon the world his superficial opinions in opposition to the settled convictions and experience of the native? I can fancy the feelings of the "lonely goatherd," who accompanied Coleridge to see the sun rise over the vale of Chamonix, when S. T. C. no doubt began to spout, as he always did. "Ah its all very well, Monsieur, to talk of 'Sovran Blanc' and all those fine things, but when the avalanches are lively about here you'l think of something else. Of course its very ennobling; but there's my boy Bibi—he's a cretin, Monsieur; that's the effect of Mont Blanc upon him; and there's Gretchen's Goitre,—that's the effect upon her!" If the author of Christabel had just then fallen accidentally down a crevasse, who could have blamed the lonely goatherd?

Between the Coast mountains in the vicinity of San Francisco, say within the compass of 100 miles north and south, lie the most fertile valleys of the state. The valley of Santa Clara, almost triangular, with its base resting upon the bay of San Francisco, its apex narrowing as the two ranges of the Coast mountains approach each other, would be the "garden spot" of California if any locality in the state could justly claim the degree of cultivation expressed by that term. The soil is rich to marvelousness. As you enter the valley, an odor as of quickening vegetation, which seems to practically express the generous qualities of the soil, but which is a pungency actually borrowed from the wild mustard, strikes your sense. On either side of the road acres on acres of golden wheat, in size that dwarfs the finest eastern crop, stretch away to the foot hills far as the eye can reach. In the fields huge machines creep slowly along, carrying in the complex operations of the harvest, —reaping, threshing, cradling, winnowing and sacking,—as they advance. These monsters, which move like vast ruminants feeding at will upon the plain, are the only signs of harvesting. There are no gleaners, reapers, piled sheaves, wagons or barns. The poetry of the harvest is gone. Agriculture here is a purely mechanical, practical operation. You look in vain for the farm house, with its comfortable surroundings, its orchard, garden, outhouses and barn. A few sheds thrust together in one corner of the field serve as a shelter for the farmer (?) and his hands. His meat and vegetables are purchased in town; his very milk and butter come from another's dairy. Harvest over, he goes to town, and the land, squeezed of its fatness, lies neglected, uncared for and forgotten.

There are of course exceptions to the foregoing, and I have seen some neat farm-houses whose tasteful gardens and accessories reminded one of the East. But they are rare. The reasons why they are exceptions are various. The land is often rented by the year to small farmers who endeavor to make the most out of the smallest outlay. The uncertainty of land titles, which prevent improvements; the fact that most of the "rancheros" find it more profitable to have their specialities; one raising wheat exclusively, another potatoes, another keeping a dairy, another a stock ranch, vine-yard or kitchen garden, but seldom combining these occupations in one,—are some of the excuses for this singular style of farming. Thus even with this prolific soil and rare climate the country looks uncultivated. It is with a feeling of relief that you at last enter the city of San Jose, through its pleasant lands and leafy approaches, its trim gardens, its neat villas and its deliciously soft atmosphere. Here is that pleasant mingling of provincial freshness and sincerity with urban taste which makes this inland town the most attractive of any in the state. Here is that paragon of excellence, the Auzerais House—a country hotel that blends the refinement, luxury and elegance of the great city caravanseries, with the healthfulness, coolness, cleanliness, breadth and liberality of the country, and which has no superior outside of San Francisco and few equals there. I know of no more pleasant surprise to the weary traveler than his first sensation on entering its broad cool halls and spacious staircases after his journey through the heat and dust of the valley. He seems to have carried the best part of civilization with him. Here is the pure country air, the rural outlook from window and piazza, and here also are the thousand conveniences of city life, which he was supposed to leave behind him. I know of no luxury that is not at his disposal. He may even have the Springfield Republican, which is taken by the host, whose wife hails from that goodly Massachusetts village. May she pardon the stranger who takes this opportunity to commend her and her husband to the pleasant remembrances and proud regards of her fellow townsmen. F.B.H.

LETTER 34

Springfield Republican, 4 September 1867
Springfield Weekly Republican, 7 September 1867

FROM CALIFORNIA.

The Exciting Political Campaign—Three Tickets before the People—The Birth and Life of the Union Party—Its Prospective Demise and Its Successor.

[From Our Special Correspondent.]

San Francisco, August 9, 1867.

For the past two months the energies of this impulsive people have been completely given up to politics. Mining stocks, speculations, the new exchange, new immigration schemes, the cholera, yellow fever and the weather, are topics that are speedily absorbed and forgotten

in the scandal elicited by the gubernatorial canvass. The Sacramento
Union, and San Francisco Bulletin and Call—the three most influential and independent papers of the state—have fought the candidate of the dominant politicians, against the "leashed thunders" of the
party press, the Alta California and Times, not to speak of the "Tray,
Blanche and Sweetheart" of interior journalism. Editorials, reports
of meetings, conventions and political correspondence have occupied
their columns to the exclusion of all else. On the other hand many of
the political meetings have been convened apparently for the purpose
of denouncing the independent press, and the Union orators have
poured out their vials of wrath on the Bulletin, Union and Call as un-
sparingly as they ever did on the heads of the democrats. The wordy
warfare has been conducted thus far with more dignity on the part
of the seceding journals than on the part of the politicians, while the
smaller party papers have indulged in an asperity whose shrillness was
in inverse ratio to their size and circulation. The politicians answer the
charges of fraud and corruption by counter charges of "treason" and
party treachery. No accusation is too absurd or too reckless. When Mr
Gorham, the gubernatorial candidate of the Union party, was lately
addressing a meeting at Placerville, he was interrupted in his arraign-
ment of the Sacramento Union by a voice from the crowd suggesting
"Democratic Union" as a more appropriate title for the paper. Mr
Gorham accepted the amended title amid great enthusiasm. When the
readers of The Republican are told that the Union is and always has
been the exponent of the radical wing of the Union party, the most
intensely anti-Johnson paper in the state, they will understand the perfect recklessness of the accusation. Yet it is no more absurd than many
of the charges which any opposition to the personelle of the Union
candidates have provoked.

The more practical effects of the division have been shown in a re-
vision of the state ticket by a convention of the disaffected, and the
placing of Bidwell at the head of the ticket, instead of Gorham. But
Bidwell having been before the regular convention which nominated
Gorham, although chagrined by his unfair defeat, feels that he cannot
with propriety accept. Caleb T. Fay, another old republican, has taken
his place and accepted the nomination of the opposition. He will not,
however, exert the influence of Bidwell, who is undoubtedly the choice
of the Union voters, and whose nomination would be a moral rebuke
to the intriguers and schemers who once defeated him. At present

there are three tickets: the regular Union nomination with Gorham at its head, the opposition styled the "national republican" with Caleb T. Fay for governor, and the regular democratic, with Henry Haight leading the usual jaded political hacks of this obsolete organization. Mr Haight is an old republican who deserted the party at the time of the emancipation proclamation. He has been a moderate politician, undemonstrative, and of considerable personal popularity. Unlike other democratic leaders he did little during the rebellion to outrage the sentiment of Union men; and but for an unfortunate speech in which he attacked President Lincoln, he might now receive many Union votes which cannot be cast for Gorham. It is true that John Conness, our Union senator, once alluded to Mr Lincoln as a "third rate clown in a third rate circus," and otherwise abused him, even while representing the Union sentiment of California, but we forgive these amiable eccentricities much more freely in a friend than an enemy. The difference between Mr Haight and Mr Gorham may be briefly summed up in a sentence. Mr Haight is a recent democrat who has not forgotten his former republican education and propriety, while Mr Gorham is a recent republican who carries into the party his former democratic training, antecedents and defeats.

The real political struggle of 1867 in California is not between the democracy and the Union party, but between the men who have attempted to rule the latter and the people. The Union party is moribund. Even the election of Gorham will not restore its waning vitality. It was born with the rebellion, it cannot outlive it, or adjust itself to new conditions. Its history is brief, but memorable. It was the offspring of the great Union meeting of the 22d of February, 1861, in San Francisco. Men of all classes and conditions, of all sections and parties, enlisted in its ranks. Local issues, party spites and jealousies were forgotten in the all absorbing principle of sustaining the supremacy of the nation. Probably in the history of politics never was a more unselfish, patriotic organization. The only opposition were those democrats who still boldly advocated secession and states' rights, and to whom the epithets of "copperheads" were perhaps more justly applied than is usual. The issue was squarely drawn. Twice was the unity of the party tried: once by the peace movement led by Senator Latham, once by the emancipation proclamation. But Thomas Starr King and a few kindred spirits boldly lifted the people over these new questions, which for a moment startled the more conservative. As the organization increased in strength and power it had many new accessions. As the national skies brightened it was noticed that the zeal of the latest converts became more intense, and a survey of the party at the close of the rebellion showed that its executive control had passed entirely into the hands of politicians, many of whom were unknown to the people at the time of its organization, or if known were of doubtful Union antecedents. Sunshine and warmth had begotten corruption in this heterogeneous mass; the body politic swarmed with political maggots. The majority of the people, no longer excited by the war, relaxed their vigilance and returned to their various peaceful callings. Politics was not their trade nor taste; and as was audaciously, but truly said, in reference to the last primary election by one of Gorham's own friends, "the business men of San Francisco lost the election because they were afraid their soup would get cold, and couldn't stay at the polls." The few who remained in the party saw too much to criticise, and met with too great opposition. The municipal elections of San Francisco, controlled since the vigilance committee by the business men of the city, were claimed by the Union party, and unprincipled demagogues and shoulder-strikers demanded office in the sacred name of the Union. To-day the same privileges are demanded for the gubernatorial campaign in the same sacred name with the added conjuration of "reconstruction according to Congress."

The decease of the Union party of California will be traced primarily to corruption. Even with its diverse integral elements it preserved its unity sufficiently to carry the state on the question of congressional reconstruction. It was the dominant party, and as such could have retained its prestige. It could have dodged the suffrage question, —here rendered peculiarly difficult by our Chinese population,—for a while, or have effected some compromise. But just now it is dying, and people are ready to hail its successor, the national republican party of California. F.B.H.

LETTER 35

Springfield Republican, 12 October 1867
Springfield Weekly Republican, 19 October 1867

FROM CALIFORNIA.

Home Productions of the Golden State—Two New Books—A Genuine Poet.

[From Our Special Correspondent.]

San Francisco, September 17, 1867.

At our present rate of progress we shall soon be completely independent of eastern manufactures and foreign products. We have already "California made" boots, hats, cloths, furniture, pianos, wines and cigars. We have public spirited citizens who, from the same noble impulse which forced the lamented Kirby to enwrap himself in the American flag without reference to its deficiencies as a becoming garment, array themselves in "Mission" woolens, drink native wines with a lofty disregard of flatulency and eructation, smoke native tobacco rolled into cigars by the long, dexterous fingers of the Mongolian, and sleep on mattresses of pulse from the Sandwich Islands, which may already be looked upon as our own territory. But these are exceptions. Californians generally are noted for their cosmopolitan tastes, and they tax the further East and West for their luxuries. We really consume but little of our own products, and most of our home made articles are more ingenious than profitable. California, from her gold fields to her manufactories, is a country of prodigal giving; we produce more than we consume; we give out more than we absorb; we pay for more than we use, and manage to keep up a vast credit in our account with the rest of the world.

The latest home-made productions are California books. We have long had a California literature. We have given to the world Phœnix, Mark Twain, and a galaxy of lesser luminaries. We have given birth to several incipient "Pacific Monthlies," two or three critical literary papers, a comic rival of Vanity Fair, y'clept Puck, and a vast number of ephemeral first-class dailies. But the Pacific monthlies came to a pacific end, the literary papers became scrofulous through defective circulation, and went off in hectic fevers. Puck got few subscribers in a community where Bottom has such a large representation, and the first-class dailies didn't succeed. It was the old trouble of inadequate demand and supply. We have in fact more writers than readers; more contributors than subscribers. Our population contains more than the average proportion of undeniably clever men, but we lack that large middle class of mediocre but appreciative folk who form the vast body of Eastern readers. Here men are too sagacious or too stupid to patronize home literature; that kind of writing which should appeal to the better class enters at once into hopeless competition with the best Eastern periodicals which are taken here, and between too much "Boston" on the one hand and too much "Pike" on the other, literature falls to the ground.

Perhaps, to look a little deeper, the exciting nature of California pursuits and pleasures are not calculated to foster anything but sensational writing. Californians, like the Arabian Prince, prefer their cream tarts with pepper. The better educated class of old and young bachelors find their enjoyments at clubs, where their literary appetite is satisfied by hasty mouthsfull of review and foreign eclectic. Again, the eminently practical and material—which is a peculiar element of our civilization—is not well adapted to encourage literature. Some years ago the state offered a premium for the first California book on the subject of California resources, printed with California-made type on California-made paper, sewn with California thread, &c., &c., *usque ad nauseam*. A very good work on the required thesis—in fact the only one of any authority extant, was published by J. S. Hittell, but it was deficient in the intrinsic quality of being made of California material and it didn't get the prize. I understand that the gentleman now proposes to republish the work, with these deficiences made good. I hope he may get the premium for the benefit of literature. One trembles to think, however, of the fate of this venture, should a foreign substance mingle with the paste, or anything mar the indigenous quality of the glue. A great state's patronage of literature hangs up on a single thread of California manufacture.

Two noteworthy books have lately been published by A. Roman & Co: "Confucius and the Chinese Classics," and "The Poems of Charles Warren Stoddard." The first is probably more of a compliment to our

Chinese population than a response to any demand of Californians to know more about the ethics of their Asiatic neighbors. It contains the pith of Legge's three volumes in one. It was edited and compiled by Rev Mr Loomis of San Francisco, but for many years a Chinese missionary. Mr Loomis has done his work well, and if he could have but forgotten that he had been a Chinese missionary, would have done it better. He cannot resist the opportunity of making a theological point in his commentary, and of endeavoring to correct any proselyting effect of the text by suitable annotation. Yet the compilation gives a very respectable idea of the teachings of this Asiatic moralist, of whom so much is said and so little known. I wonder how many of the clever folk who allude to Confucius have ever read him. To how many is he as vague and intangible as Haroun Al Raschid or Kubla Khan? Lo, here he is, resurrected in San Francisco, A.D. 1867, in his "robes of ceremony," with the faint odor of sacrifice about him, and that awful sententiousness which has survived centuries. Behold him—the precise, fastidious, superstitious old moralist, who "never was without ginger when he ate," who "did not eat meat that was not cut properly, nor what was served without its proper sauce," who "required his sleeping dress to be half as long again as his body," who "if his mat was not straight would not sit on it," who, "when he was fasting, changed the place where he commonly sat in the apartment," who "changed countenance" at "a clap of thunder, a violent wind," or when his prince spoke to him. Behold those famous political and moral sayings of this strange combination of prime minister and philosopher—this Chinese mingling of Richelieu and Socrates. Here are those apothegms, so broad, so catholic, so liberal, that one looks with wonder on the narrow, mean, selfish and superstitious race who have brought them down through history. Here are the Chinese classics comprising Mencius, Confucius, Buddhist tracts and poetry—the profound wisdom of the ancient East, composed, stereotyped, printed and bound in this modern city of the West—the oldest book and the newest publication. This is something noteworthy, if the book had no other merits. But the Riverside press could hardly offer a neater, more tasteful specimen of book-work than this California maiden venture.

What effect this comprehensive way of introducing us to the social and moral inner life of the Chinese will have upon our relations with their country—which is just at present purely mercenary and selfish on our part—I cannot say. I am afraid that a good translation of Chinese statistics, or an accurate commercial dictionary would acquire a quicker circulation than Confucius. I can hardly conceive that our merchants would be apt to quote him to their Chinese customers, or that his ethics would obtain generally in Sacramento or Front street.

The "Poems of Charles Warren Stoddard" are more correctly a California production. The poet is young, and his education, training and experience have been Californian, but it is his chief merit that this modest little volume contains no trace of that fact. The hardness, skepticism and Philistinism of life on this coast have not touched him. How he has kept alive this sacred vestal flame, how he has remained faithful to this one shrine where there are so many altars, how he has kept his wings unsoiled, and his singing robes clean in contact with the dust and dirt of this fast community, and how he has preserved the serene repose of the true poet amid all this twitter, whirl and excitement, are secrets that even the frank confession of his verse leaves untold. Among the tuneful mob, his pure young voice rises the one clear, sustained, heaven-born note. We have native singers enough,— Heaven help us,—as we have California canaries, but this one who

> "Sings of what the world will be
> When the years have died away,"

Can he be Californian? Who taught this young jackanapes to sin against the recognized California canon that poetry is a kind of mental dissipation checked by meter and kept in bounds by rhyme? On what hasheesh or "mystic drug" has he been fed that, in this sharp sunlight, this "pert" atmosphere, he falls into a trance and has visions of what he calls

> "the heavy dusks that gloom
> The groves of spice beyond the seas."

Who taught the young varlet such graphic simplicity of statement as

> "the fitful puffs that fret
> The eternal levels of the sea."

in a country where metaphors are simple extravagance and slang. Surely this poet was born, and not made,—we at least had no hand in shaping him. Or if the quickening influence of soil and climate which give us peach trees, four feet high, that bear in their second year, have given us premature fruit from this young fellow of one and twenty, is the fruit fully ripe? Try one of the specimens before us:—

DRIFTING.

A lark's song rippled in the air,
　　With liquid trill that smote the dawn,
　　He hastened down the dewy lawn
And found the morning breezes fair;

And half the anchor-cable in,
　　And half the sails were loosed, and full
　　Of salty winds; with steady pull
He bade the frothing eddies spin

And whirl about his dripping oar,
　　As on he sped and joined the bark;
　　Then from the deck he leaned to mark
The wondrous beauty of the shore.

They seemed as falling scales, his tears,
　　From blinded eyes, that would not see
　　How comfort in that home could be,
Though comfort kept him all his years.

High on the yard a sailor sang:
　　"O! dusky love beyond the sea!
　　O! dusky love that longs for me"—
"And thee," the mocking echoes rang.

"There is a glory in the gale—
　　An idle dream will suit the calm,
　　And talk of leafy thatch and palm—
Shall fill the watch with song and tale.

"Lo! yonder is the star that guides
　　The mariner; we lift our hands
　　About the world in many lands;
For what are winds and what are tides,

"But spirits luring us abroad?
　　Rise fragrant isles before our eyes—
　　A pyre for passion's sacrifice,
Where pleasure is our only god!"

* * * * *

A hundred trilling songs of larks
A hundred blooming dawns may greet
But who shall stay the wanderer's feet,
And call his spirit from the dark?

Surely there is no immateriality here. Neither is there any provincial flavor. Wherever that poem grew, its roots struck deeper than our superficial civilization. These may be imitations, but the model is good, and the similarity is only one of attitude and mood. But I am trespassing on the ground of your reviewer, and this reminds me that our California poet, (who is not Californian,) has received a cordial welcome from the press here. The Bulletin gives him a genial, appreciative notice, and the Californian, a weekly literary paper, would have done the like I think, had it not attempted to prove in the same article that California possessed a critic as well as poet.   F.B.H.

LETTER 36

Springfield Republican, 4 November 1867

FROM CALIFORNIA.

Hell Definitely Located and Staked Out—A Japanese Showman Astonishes a
San Francisco Audience—The "Outside Land" Question—Return of the
Telegraph Exploring Expedition—The College of California Dead.

[From Our Special Correspondent.]
San Francisco, October 8, 1867.

Orthodox readers of The Republican will be glad to know that hell has been at last definitely located. The honor of the discovery belongs to the Pacific slope and the Montana Post. The head waters of the Yellowstone river is the locality indicated. As this is only reached by going through Montana, the infernal conditions seem to be perfect.

According to the Post, it appears that a party of explorers, being for eight days overborne by a multiplicity of frightful stenches, sulphurous fumes, belching volcanoes, springs of boiling nitric acid (chemically pure), and "living brimstone rivers," at once recognized the spot, and gave it the significant title of "Hell." What these men saw there I shudder to transcribe in detail; yet amidst these terrors they moved on calm and undaunted. With the fearless courage of the Montanan prospector they gave a title to the locality, quietly staked off their lots, pre-empted Hell, and on their return formally filed their certificates in the clerk's office. The subject is one which invites the serious attention of religious professors. What possible hold can the orthodox scheme of future punishment have upon such a people? How feeble must the imagination of even the revivalist Earle appear beside this genuine Montanan exhibition.

The near fact is that we live in a country unpleasantly new and uncomfortably inchoate. Even the advantage of personally inspecting and recording the genesis of creation cannot compensate us for all the inconveniencies. Our earthquakes are already recognized as part of the system, but it is hard that to the chaotic state of civilization about Montana, nature should add her terrors. One would think that infamous whisky and Indian arrows were bad enough, without brimstone and Indian arrows being superadded. But nature partakes of the general lawlessness, and, sitting by the wayside, levies her tax on the unlucky Montanan, conjointly with road agents and savages. Trifles like these do not, however, discourage the true pioneer. Tenants are ready to occupy the house before it is finished or the scaffolding removed. They are even willing to suggest alterations or improvements, and doubtless there exists the intelligent Montanan who is competent to assist and accelerate nature on the Yellowstone with a little nitro glycerine.

A Japanese episode, the other day, afforded some gossip for the town. A troupe of jugglers, a recent importation direct from Japan, were announced to far exceed any of their professional brethren who had previously performed here. They were under the charge of one "Hi-ya-ti-kee"—an obstinate, self-opinionated and perfectly independent Japanese, yet possessing great dexterity and skill withal. Hi-ya-ti-kee could receive no suggestions from outside barbarians, would take no advice, could be taught nothing. To all interference or counsel he invariably responded, "I am Hi-ya-ti-kee," with a lofty superiority and imperious eloquence of gesture that abashed our most audacious local showmen. There was really something sublime in this old heathen's sententiousness and independence. Every one yielded—he had everything his own way, even to employing his own native carpenters, who, with the tools of "forty centuries," laboriously put the stage in order, and in one week completed that which a Yankee carpenter would have finished in a day. Notwithstanding this awful preparation and precision the first performance was hardly a success. Hi-ya-ti-kee, in spite of his cleverness, was a good deal of a bore with his formalities and dignified preludes, another member of the troupe, who talked incessantly and acted as a kind of Greek chorus, was also tedious, and the orchestra, composed solely of Japanese drummers and fiddlers, was insufferable. But a few evenings later the sensation came. One of the tricks—and a very ingenious one—was the spinning of two large tops which ascended an inclined plane, and then opened, disclosing, the one, a rabbit which Hi-ya-ti-kee exhibited to the audience, and the other—but here I must seek safety in a periphrasis. You remember, my dear Republican, certain ornaments which adorned the houses of the good people of Pompeii previous to the destruction of that literal city, and which survived the ruins only to be locked up in the museum at Naples where they now lie. Well, the other top disclosed what a prudish Neapolitan government to-day takes such pains to conceal. The dress circle, composed of gentlemen and ladies, were both stupefied and shocked. The galleries, not being able to trace the progress of Phallic worship from the Romans to the Japanese, accepted the fact as an original vulgarity unauthorized by precedent or custom, and were at once delighted and indignant. In spite of the disgust, perfect bewilderment and indignation inspired by the scene, there was something inexpressibly grotesque in the contrasted demeanor of these two civilizations, brought face to face with each other, and suddenly awakened to a knowledge of the impassable gulf between. Blissfully unconscious of aught but a light Japanese pleasantry, Hi-ya-ti-kee had walked to the foot-lights and displayed with the calmness of a Heller or Anderson, what in their hands would probably have been a baby's cap or other professionally funny article. Our friend of the Greek chorus took the opportunity to explain in Japanese the full importance of the symbol, the orchestra struck up a lively Japanese air and the musicians themselves—Japanese ladies—sang an epithalmium. The petrified audience could not dodge the fact. Some few rose to leave the house, some audibly expressed their disgust, but a majority were astonished to silence. The next night Hi-ya-ti-kee consented to receive advice in regard to his performances.

The city "outside land" question is beginning to assume a serious aspect. You doubtless remember that the city's "Pueblo" title to her outside lands, now occupied by bona fide settlers and purchasers, has been confirmed. Under the old Mexican law by which she claimed the title, the land was to be simply held in trust for her citizens and issued to them in lots for actual occupation. The "homeless" and "landless" folk of San Francisco now claim that the lands should be given up to them on application, that every one should have a homestead for the asking, and that rich owners of large tracts and all but bona fide settlers should be dispossessed. According to the law, they allege no man can claim more than a certain sized lot, and then only for actual occupation. A good many sensible men really believe that this will be done, and some enterprising fellows have made it profitable to draw applications at the rate of $5 each, which are duly filed in the clerk's office. Unfortunately, action has not been confined to this innocent formality. Attempts have been made to "squat" and "jump" lots, and already serious riot and bloodshed have ensued. An authoritative and final settlement of the question is criminally delayed, partly because local politics are beginning to mingle with it. The "Pueblo land organization" is a large body of voters and candidates, and officials must trim their sails accordingly. We shall be fortunate if the matter is not pushed to final arbitrament by violent disturbances. A serious defect of this people is their disposition to trifle with the grave conditions of their civilisation—edged tools that won't bear reckless handling.

The Russian-American—called, I think, the "Western Union"—telegraph company, having temporarily abandoned their enterprise, returned their employes to San Francisco a day or two ago, by the "Nightingale" from Alaska. The story of these men, who for three years had led a wild and precarious existence on the extreme northwestern shelf of the continent, is full of romantic interest. Doubtless their adventures will in due time be properly told. Like most of the Arctic expeditions, this is at present the only result. Polar explorations have so far only supplied the demand for the marvellous and sensational. On this side of the continent, ice is the only practical thing we get from the frigid zone.

The college of California, after a long and protracted struggle for life, gave up the ghost yesterday, and dissolved its organization, making over its property to the state for an agricultural college. I have neither the time nor temper to-day to discuss the causes which led to this shameful result, but in my next shall speak more plainly than I have ever done before of what must be called the moral and intellectual degeneracy of this country.   H.

LETTER 37

Christian Register, 28 December 1867

[From our Regular Correspondent.]

CALIFORNIA.

San Francisco, Nov. 12, 1867.

SUNDAY IN SAN FRANCISCO.

Even in this restless community the seventh day brings the usual Sabbath transformation and quietude. Whether it is part of that fancy with which we are so apt to delude ourselves, that Nature participates in the holiday, and wears a more benignant and smiling aspect, I cannot say, but even here, the sunlight seems to have become more mellowed and tender, the air less harsh and irritating, the bay more smooth and shining, and the hard outlines of the distant hills less salient. The streets, too, have a Sabbath cleanliness—a cleanliness here, however, begotten of a dry atmosphere where the wind performs the office of street sweeper and scavenger. The people you meet partake of this outward semblance of purity and regeneration, for San Francisco is proverbially a well-dressed city. Even the stranger, who accosts you with the request for money to buy his breakfast, wears spotless linen, the spendthrift or bankrupt contemplating suicide to-morrow, to-day at least passes you in carefully brushed broadcloth. It may be parenthetically remarked here as a kind of illustration of our habits, that according to a rude, unwritten code of propriety and honor, few Californians permit themselves to sink into the seedy stage of poverty—estopping by crime or suicide that humiliating condition. So tacitly is this recognized that the few beggars who appear on the streets and flout their rags in the true mendicant style, are promptly arrested as imposters.

The order and individual decorum of a San Francisco Sabbath is very apt to strike a stranger with astonishment. With all our laxity of principle, foreign habits and perfect freedom and license, there are fewer rowdies and drunkards seen in the streets on that day than in any other city of the Union. With a large non-church-going population, with several gardens open to the pleasure-seeker, with target excursions, fast driving and base-ball gymnastics in the public squares, there is no public disturbance or boisterousness, and the police arrests do not exceed the other days. You walk out this pleasant Sabbath morning, and are passing one of the principal churches just as the congregation is being dismissed. The organ is still playing, but above its swell suddenly rises the blare of martial music. Down the street, with colors flying, marches a German rifle company. The doxology perhaps contends for a few moments with the strains of Von Weber, and the waltz and brass instruments triumph. The two parties meet face to face and eye each other curiously. Beyond a certain self-satisfied air of successful competition on the countenances of each the rencounter produces no effect. It is true that when the band passes the church during service one is apt to lose the words of the officiating minister, but as there are some statements of theology in which this interruption is not altogether objectionable I don't know that much harm is done. It depends a good deal upon the preacher.

Fond as San Franciscans are of fast driving, the display is confined entirely to the suburbs of the city, and the Sunday quiet is broken only by the horse-cars. The lines which lead to the suburban places of resort are most patronized, and here the stranger gets a fair idea of the proportion of Sabbath pleasure-seekers to Sabbath church-goers. All day long the cars running to the Mission, Hayes' Park, City Gardens and Woodworth's Gardens are crowded. Touching these latter places, it must be confessed that on purely æsthetic grounds the churches are preferable. There is very little rural simplicity about the Gardens, and the poetical excuse for Sabbath breaking in the country can hardly obtain on this sandy peninsular where Nature is so uncomely, and her works so frightfully artificial. The proportion of bowling alleys, restaurants, swings, gymnastic ladders and other appliances for active material enjoyment is so great as to exclude the idea of any very extensive religious meditation. When I say the churches are æsthetically superior,—more real, truthful and natural,—I, of course, do not limit myself to their external appurtenants. Heaven forefend that I should insinuate that there was anything at any time scenic, artificial or magnificent in their services or teachings. Architecturally they are fine, although inferior in point of taste to the banks, insurance offices and hotels; still this is an improvement in a community where five years ago the decorative art was exclusively lavished upon engine houses. The two most solidly built churches are the Unitarian and the Jewish Synagogue. The former is the poorest in style of any. Although large it is so well proportioned as to lead the observer to under-estimate its size; it suggests a chapel rather than a church, or of being the perfect porch of some more stately edifice as yet unseen. I have sometimes thought that perhaps this idea might have been in the mind of its noble founder—a part of the work unfinished by Mr. King when he laid himself down to eternal rest in its shadow. The interior of the Jewish Synagogue bears away the palm for costly and luxurious decoration. The Catholic Cathedral and Grace Church or "Grace Cathedral" as the Episcopal Bishop loves to call it, are equally ambitious, but are both unfinished in the matter of spires, and while they are complete where they touch the ground, they are more or less defective when they approximate to the heavens. This is especially true of the new Trinity (Episcopal) Church—a finely designed Norman-gothic edifice of wood, whose sham walls of Oregon pine are upheld by equally insincere buttresses of tongued-and-grooved redwood. Here the spire, which seems to have gotten fairly under way—like some original conception of Christianity—suddenly stops short, and throws up from one corner the feeblest little spire or spirelet imaginable, artificial, attenuated and ridiculous, leaving the original broad foundation bare—the general effect being that of a very slim lightning rod on a very broad chimney. Indeed some of the churches are stingy on the subject of spires—doubtless owing to the insecurity of a soil subject to terrestrial spasms. The Methodist Church on Howard street, has two extraordinary additions to its towers, which look like *antennæ* and make the whole building resemble an insect—a resemblance the more striking, during an earthquake, when the "feelers" are endowed with singular vitality. I hesitate to dwell upon the rare perfections of Dr. Wadsworth's (Presbyterian) or Dr. Stone's (Congregationalist) Church; suffice it to say that they express the concrete New England idea of a "meeting house." Where else can you find that general flam of a town-

hall, Greek temple, merchant's exchange, and cheap lecture-room?
Where else can you find that cold, white, rectangular apartment with
its rigid division of pews, its broad, semicircular sweep as if made by
the mason's trowel just behind the reading-desk, its chilly galleries
over which many a Sunday-school scholar has leaned and wildly con-
templated suicide as a means of "fleeing from the wrath to come," its
high steps to make room for that dreadful basement, wherein good
children are confined in company with the Hebrew prophets and the
uninteresting Kings of the Old Testament. I shudder as I pass the spot,
and feel like rushing in to make a general jail-delivery of the unhappy
innocents who pensively look at me through the windows.

There is a church which I have not yet described, but which, more
than any other perhaps, has a local California flavor. It looks not unlike a theatre, but possesses this advantage over the buildings I have
just enumerated—being really what it appears—nothing more nor less
than a theatre. Supposing the reader has accompanied me thus far,
we will look at it a little more closely. It is almost eight o'clock; the
elaborate, social, San Francisco Sunday dinner—that dreadful meal
anathematized by Bishop Kip and bewailed by Dr. Stone—is just over,
and a selfish, good-humored crowd are turned loose upon the streets
to digest their repast and smoke their cigars. The doors of the theatre
are open; we follow the crowd that seems to be setting in that direction
and enter. It is quite early yet, but the building is crowded already
from pit to dome. Men predominate, although in the dress circle there
is a sprinkling of well-dressed and respectable appearing women. A
few new-comers stand near the door, with California prudence keeping their line of retreat open and not committing themselves to the
service by taking a seat. Glance around at the faces—all of them intelligent, many refined and cultured. Taking the different degrees of
dress and breeding as a criterion it is a pretty fair representation of
the *people*. You can distinguish those who have not been here before
by their half-supercilious, wholly critical air. A tall, strongly built man
now steps upon the stage and advances to the footlights. The face
he turns upon the audience is full of strength—unclerical, as popular
ideas go, in its suggestion of radical practical power. Its salient outlines seem to have been shaped more by contact with humanity than
theology. His chin and mouth are resolute and decisive although their
sternness is relieved by long, flowing, English side-whiskers. It is only
when he speaks, that his voice, deep, earnest and thoughtful, shows
him to be a thinker as well as a man of affairs. He says a few simple

words and every one becomes attentive. By the time he has finished the sentence he has established a personal relation with each one of his auditors. His tone, his words, his hearty recognition of their manhood, his freedom from cant and sentimentalism have irresistibly won them. He makes a broad statement of religion without having recourse to a single professional term. He makes a clean proposition—free from clerical slang, and submits it to his hearers as if it were really something within the domain of their reasoning faculties. He seems to speak the unspoken thought of each man's breast—the doubts, fears, aspirations and ambitions of the soul, all that men usually hide, smother or transform when they come before the altar, he voices to-night. "You have within you," he says, "the seeds of all that you require in religion —all that you want to understand Christianity—if you are only true to yourselves." The men who have been standing near the door have quietly dropped into seats and have allowed their retreat to be cut off; the supercilious look has been changed into one of interest, the last comer nearest the passage way, who had retained his accustomed cigar in his fingers, throws it away and makes up his mind to stay five minutes longer. Assuredly this Truth is a wonderful thing. It has drawn such audiences as we see here before us every Sunday evening since the services were commenced; it will continue to draw them as long as this preacher or any other shall have the manliness and love for Truth to speak in its behalf. Wonderful principle, that has transformed these material, skeptical, selfish, and easy-going Sabbath breakers into regular church attendants—for that is what this assemblage means. The speaker proceeds with his discourse—the audience would applaud, but are restrained, not by the thought of the edifice but, better, by the deep, reverential sentiment that now fills them, and transfigures even the cheap gilding of this worldly temple. The speaker has spoken truly. The Sabbath was made for man; the shrine for the worshipper. As he inspires it only is the day or the temple holy or sacred.

The audience just dismissed are earnest, thoughtful but not reserved. They look bright and cheerful. As one of them quotes with gusto some remark of the preacher, the other says, with an earnestness and feeling which makes us forget the irreverence, "Bully for Stebb!" "Stebb," my dear *Register*, is the *Californian* for the Rev. Dr. Stebbins, pastor of the Unitarian church, the only minister who in this country of orthodox revivals and prayer meetings, has really stirred the deep popular heart into religious enthusiasm and awakened Christianity.

H.

L E T T E R   1 . Harte repeatedly uses the abbreviations "ult." and "inst." in these letters to refer to the previous (or ultimate) and present (or instant) month.

According to a contemporary report, the pews in the First Unitarian Church of San Francisco "are not owned by individuals, but belong to the Society, whose organic law requires that they shall be rented annually to the highest bidder" ("The First Unitarian Church," San Francisco *Alta California*, 31 March 1867, 2:2–3).

Harte replies in this letter to Henry W. Bellows's recent suggestion that "our Unitarian friends on the Pacific coast" exploit "the opportunity of planting another church of our faith in San Francisco!" ("Our Prospects in California," *Christian Register*, 7 October 1865, p. 157).

Thomas Starr King (1824–1864) arrived in San Francisco in April 1860. The cornerstone of the Gothic-style church, located on the south side of Geary street, near Stockton, was laid in December 1862. The building was formally dedicated in January 1864, less than two months before King's sudden death. On King, see Charles W. Wendte, *Thomas Starr King: Patriot and Preacher* (Boston: Beacon, 1921); and Kevin Starr, *Americans and the California Dream 1850–1915* (New York: Oxford University Press, 1973), pp. 97–105. Horatio Stebbins (1821–1902) had served as the Unitarian minister in Portland, Maine, from 1859 until his call to San Francisco in 1864. Charles G. Ames (1828–1912) arrived in California in the fall of 1865, as Bellows later wrote, "to reenforce Mr. Stebbins, so far as he may need or be disposed to accept relief in his labors, and to do general missionary service on the Pacific coast." He later contributed to the *Overland Monthly*, 2 (April 1869), 359–63; and 2 (June 1869), 545–51; and he remained in California until 1872. The lives of each of these three Unitarian clergymen are sketched in the *Dictionary of American Biography*.

In addition to serving as Superintendent of the U. S. Mint and chairman of the Board of Trustees of the First Unitarian Society, Robert B. Swain (1822–1872) was president of the local Mercantile Library Association. Harte refers to his *Address before the First Unitarian Society of San Francisco, in memory of their late pastor, Rev. Thomas Starr King, March 15, 1864* (San Francisco: Eastman, 1864).

LETTER 2. Harte slightly misquotes Prospero in *The Tempest*, act iv, scene i, line 155; and he alludes later in the letter to *Macbeth*.

LETTER 3. A. L. Stone, pastor of the Park Street Church in Boston for seventeen years, succeeded E. J. Lacey as minister of the First Congregational Church at the corner of California and Dupont streets in San Francisco. He was formally installed on 14 June 1866 (San Francisco *Bulletin*, 15 June 1866, 3:3).

To the consternation of the Radical Republicans, President Andrew Johnson had vetoed an act of Congress to establish a Freedman's Bureau in late February 1866 (*New York Times*, 20 February 1866, 1:1–3). Harte summarizes Stebbins's sermon on the topic.

LETTER 4. The local celebration of the Chinese New Year is reported in the San Francisco *Alta California*, 8 May 1866, 1:1. Harte refers in both this letter and the next one to Professor John W. Draper (1811–1882), a chemist and historian who had warned of the dangers of unchecked immigration in *Thoughts on the Future Civil Policy of America* (1865). Harte would also quote the same words of Shakespeare's Malvolio ("sad and civil") to describe the Chinese protagonist in his story "Wan Lee, the Pagan" (1874).

LETTER 5. An earthquake that caused little damage had occurred in the early afternoon of 26 March 1866 ("The Earthquake in the Interior," San Francisco *Alta California*, 27 March 1866, 1:5). San Francisco had suffered a severe earthquake—the most violent in its history before 1906—in the early afternoon of 8 October 1865 ("The Earthquake on Sunday," San Francisco *Call*, 10 October 1865, 1:2). Like Harte, the San Francisco *Dramatic Chronicle* minimized the threat to the future of the city: "Sensible people here smile at the ridiculous statements in regard to the panic created by the 'great earthquake'" ("Our Earthquake," 21 July 1866, 2:2).

Daniel O. McCarthy of the San Francisco *Daily American Flag* was the "editor of a violently radical and aggressive sheet" whom Harte mentions. He had been jailed for contempt on 17 February 1866 for refusing to testify before the state legislature after charging seven state senators with bribery. See also letter 32 and the notes to letter 26. The San Francisco *Bulletin* excoriated McCarthy in similar terms in "A History with a Moral" (12 July 1866, 2:2).

General R. B. Van Valkenburg, U. S. Minister to Japan, and Anson Burlingame, U. S. Minister to China, had arrived in San Francisco on 24 March 1866 and were feted at the dinner Harte mentions on 28 March 1866 (San Francisco *Alta California*, 29 March 1866, 1:2).

The reviewer of *Outcroppings* for the New York *Nation* had written that "the fervor of California suns is palpable only in the erotic nature of some of the verse" (7 November 1865, p. 724). "How absurdly ignorant you people beyond the mountains are of California," C. H. Webb responded in his correspondence with the *New York Times* (15 February 1866, 8:3–5). (Webb also criticized Harte in this column, insinuating that the editor of *Outcroppings* "threw in" a "number of verses" as "sops to the Cerberuses of the Court.") The *Nation* in turn replied to Webb on 1 March 1866, p. 258, suggesting the "San Francisco cockney" was unaware the climate of the Bay area "does not extend over the whole state." In the final paragraph of this letter, Harte sides with the *Nation* against his nemesis Webb.

LETTER 6. Harte's similar "Bohemian Paper" about the Mission Dolores had appeared in the *Golden Era* for 22 March 1863.

LETTER 7. This account of the explosion is essentially accurate, to judge from three contemporary reports, each of which begins by describing the event as "terrible," the same term Harte uses: "Terrible Calamity," San Francisco *Bulletin*, 16 April 1866, 5:5; "Terrible Calamity," San Francisco *Alta California*, 17 April 1866, 1:2–4; "Terrible Disaster," San Francisco *Examiner*, 17 April 1866, 3:3. Harte slightly misquotes a line from Longfellow's "The Psalm of Life" in the final paragraph.

LETTER 8. Harte paraphrases in this letter "How Wells, Fargo & Co. Propose to Deal with Road Agents," an article in the San Francisco *Alta California* for 18 May 1866, 1:1.

LETTER 9. Mark Twain recounts his experience in downtown San Francisco during the October 1865 earthquake in chapter 58 of *Roughing It*.

LETTER 10. The commencement program of the College of California, with an oration by the Rev. Henry M. Scudder of the Howard Presbyterian Church, had been announced in mid-May ("College of California," San Francisco *Alta California*, 12 May 1866, 1:1). Harte was elected an honorary member of the "Associated Alumni of the Pacific Coast" at its meeting in June. Andrew Williams was Harte's stepfather, and Oscar L. Shafter sat on the state Supreme Court. The graduation exercises were subsequently described in detail in both the *Alta California* (7 June 1866, 1:2) and the San Francisco *Bulletin* (7 June 1866, 3:3–4). The latter article includes summaries of Shafter's and Stebbins's orations.

The new registry law is published and its implications discussed in "Enrolment of Voters," *Alta California*, 5 June 1866, 1:2.

The American actor Edwin Forrest (1806–1872) played the title role in Edward Bulwer-Lytton's 1838 verse play "Cardinal Richelieu" at Maguire's Opera House in San Francisco on May 14, 15, 29, and June 14 and 28. Local reviewers criticized his acting in such notices as "Forrest's 'Richelieu,'" San

Francisco *Dramatic Chronicle*, 15 May 1866, 2:1; and "Edwin Forrest's 'Lear,'" San Francisco *Examiner*, 23 May 1866, 3:2. In his assessment of Forrest's mature style of performing, Harte echoes the reviewer for the *Alta California*: "Mr. Forrest has all the fire of his younger days, and a discretion and experience which probably have corrected some of the faults of his earlier efforts" (5 June 1866, 1:2). The first choice of seats to Forrest's performances were sold at auction for as much as $500 (San Francisco *Daily American Flag*, 12 May 1866, 1:3).

L E T T E R   1 1 . Stone was criticized for politicizing the issue of Sunday worship in "A Pulpit Demagogue," San Francisco *Examiner*, 18 June 1866, 3:5. The *Pacific Churchman*, the organ of the Protestant Episcopal Church on the west coast, was edited by Rev. Thomas W. Brotherton, rector of St. John's Church.

The Bishop of California whom Harte criticizes for acquiesing to slavery was William Ingraham Kip (1811–1893). See also Harte's comments on Kip in letters 23 and 26. Harte praises the Episcopal minister J. B. Hill of Sacramento for his anti-slavery stance.

St. James's Church was "the only Episcopal Church on the Pacific coast with a full choral service, which is performed by a choir of twenty boys in surplices" (*Alta California*, 24 August 1866, 1:2). Harte also mentions the church in letter 26.

L E T T E R   1 2 . The San Francisco *Bulletin* reported on 26 June 1866 (3:4) that the Committee on Arrangements for the Fourth of July had met "with some of our leading colored citizens" and mutually agreed "that, in view of the prejudice, whether just or unjust, which showed itself on the part of a portion of the people last year, it will be better for all parties that they should take no part in the celebration." Three days later, at a public meeting of black residents of San Francisco, a resolution was adopted condemning "any person or persons" who may have compromised "the right of our people to parade on the Fourth of July." The Secretary of the Committee on Arrangements replied to this resolution that "in accordance with a mutual understanding" reached earlier, "no place had been assigned them in the line" (San Francisco *Bulletin*, 30 June 1866, 5:4.)

Stone's Fourth of July oration is reprinted in its entirety in the *Bulletin* for 5 July 1866, 3:3–6. Harte refers in particular in his letter to Stone's declaration against racial exclusion, as follows: "Nor can I think it wise or generous or just to persist in the old social proscription of any whom the law has endowed with the sacred name of AMERICAN CITIZENS. That badge of CITIZENSHIP ought to be with us as illustrious a distinction, as peerless a crown as it ever was in early Rome. If we degrade [it] in another, by social outlawry, we degrade it and for ourselves. Cannot that be seen? Least of all and last of all should we do it dishonor with a race by whom it has been won through ages of suffering and by deeds of heroic valor and many a bloody day in the fields."

The *Monadnock* and *Vanderbilt* docked in San Francisco on 22 June 1866. The dismantled monitor *Camanche* had been salvaged from San Francisco bay during the summer and fall of 1864, though it would never fire its guns in battle. It eventually became a coal barge and was scraped in the 1920s (Edgar M. Branch, *Clemens of the Call* [Berkeley and Los Angeles: University of California Press, 1969], pp. 250–254). Commodore John Rodgers arrived in the *Vanderbilt* to assume command of the U. S. Pacific fleet (San Francisco *Bulletin*, 22 June 1866, 3:4). Rodgers had been roundly criticized for refusing to defend Valparaiso from a group of Spanish ships early in 1866.

William G. Ross was shot by Charley Duane on 23 May 1866 and died the next day. Ross was a one-time inspector in the Custom House. Nicknamed "Dutch Charley," Duane had been expelled from the city by the infamous Vigilance Committee in 1856, though he returned when the edict was lifted in 1861. As the *Bulletin* explained at the time of his arrest, "Since his return he has been unusually quiet, owing to the fact that he has been a cripple for several years, having been most of the time unable to walk without a heavy cane or crutch" (24 May 1866, 3:4). John Duane was arrested the day Ross died as an accessory to murder. The Duane brothers were subsequently found not guilty (San Francisco *Bulletin*, 2 November 1866, 3:5), though they were suspected of jury-tampering in the case (San Francisco *Dramatic Chronicle*, 24 October 1866, 2:1).

Forrest's holiday at the Geysers is described in detail in "Our Watering Places/Number Five," *Dramatic Chronicle*, 11 August 1866, 2:2. Nearly half of the city of Portland, Maine, had been destroyed by fire on July 4–5.

LETTER 13. For Stone's remarks on the Fourth of July, see the notes to letter 12 above. The black San Franciscans' protests of the celebration are reported in the San Francisco *Bulletin*, 5 July 1866, 3:6. The Zion Methodist Church, formerly the First Unitarian, was located on Stockton street between Clay and Sacramento.

Harte's remarks on suicide appeared during a rash of "self-murders" in the city. According to the *Bulletin*, there were twenty suicides annually in San Francisco, or "one in every 6,050 inhabitants" (25 October 1866, 2:2). The California Academy of Natural Sciences, with the distinguished geologist J. D. Whitney (1819–1896) presiding, met semi-monthly.

LETTER 14. The newsletter of the American Unitarian Association, the *Monthly Journal*, was edited and published in Boston.

LETTER 15. The circumstances surrounding the discovery of the Pliocene skull are recounted in "A Great Geological Discovery," San Francisco *Alta California*, 17 July 1866, 1:2; and in George Stewart, Jr., *Bret Harte: Argonaut and Exile* (Boston and New York: Houghton Mifflin, 1931), pp. 142–144. The discovery of the "huge iron coffer" is similarly described in "A Relic of Old Times Exhumed," *Alta California*, 31 July 1866, 1:2.

Soon after his arrival in Boston in the spring of 1871, Harte told Annie Fields, the wife of James T. Fields, the story of the block of early San Francisco houses "laid on boxes of tobacco" (M. A. DeWolfe Howe, *Memories of a Hostess* [Boston: Atlantic Monthly Press, 1922], p. 234). He also referred to the building foundations "made of boxes of plug tobacco" in lieu of "more expensive lumber" in his late essay "Bohemian Days in San Francisco."

Frederick Law Olmsted's proposal for a public park for San Francisco, dated 31 March 1866, was published in the San Francisco *Bulletin* for 10 May 1866, 1:1–5.

Harte apparently gleans the "grotesque" incident about the cadaver from a news report. See "Arrested," *Alta California*, 3 August 1866, 1:2: "Turner Cowing, who resides at No. 323 First street, was arrested yesterday morning, on the charge of misdemeanor, by maintaining a nuisance, in the shape of the remains of his wife, who died a year since. . . ." The comparison to Hawthorne is particularly apropos; Harte would review Hawthorne's *Passages from the English Note-Books* in the *Overland*, 5 (September 1870), 289–91.

LETTER 16. The account of the collapse of the building in this letter and the next one is essentially accurate, to judge from two contemporary reports, each of which begins by describing the event as "terrible," the same term Harte uses: "Terrible Calamity," San Francisco *Bulletin*, 17 August 1866, 3:4–5; and "Terrible Catastrophe," San Francisco *Alta California*, 18 August 1866, 1:2–3. According to the former article, the building had been erected in 1858 "and was considered to be substantially built."

LETTER 17. Olmstead's plan for laying out the grounds of Berkeley is summarized and excerpted in "Berkeley Neighborhood," San Francisco *Bulletin*, 8 September 1866, 5:5. See also "The New Town of Berkeley," *Bulletin*, 29 May 1866, 3:3.

LETTER 18. Eliza DeWolf, a dress reformer, was arrested on August 6 and released by Judge John Dwinelle the next day. (On Dwinelle, see also letters 21 and 32.) While the incident inspired the predictable stories on "The DeWolf in Men's Clothing" (San Francisco *Alta California*, 8 August 1866, 1:3), his action was editorially approved in "An Enlightened Decision," San Francisco *Dramatic Chronicle*, 10 August 1866, 2:2; and "Bloomerism," San Francisco

Bulletin, 23 August 1866, 2:1–2. Still, when she appeared on Montgomery street on August 17 "clad in a Bloomer suit of glaring green," DeWolf drew a crowd estimated at several hundred. "The glaring color of her dress attracted particular attention," according to one account, "and assisted materially in enabling her to gain notoriety, for which she has apparently long sought" ("Much Ado About Nothing," San Francisco *Bulletin,* 17 August 1866, 3:6; and "Getting What She Went After," *Alta California,* 17 August 1866, 1:1).

Harte excerpts Mark Twain's "A Month of Mourning" from the *Sacramento Weekly Union* for 4 August 1866; reprinted in *Letters from the Sandwich Islands,* ed. G. Ezra Dane (San Francisco: Grabhorn, 1937), pp. 116–21; and *Mark Twain's Letters from Hawaii,* ed. A. Grove Day (New York: Appleton-Century, 1966), pp. 170–75.

LETTER 19. Harte telescopes a number of recent columns into "the latest copy of the Republican." The European correspondent C.S.W. ("Over the Seas") recounted her visit to Naples in the issue for May 19 (1:2–3), for example, and the Boston correspondent Raynesford had described his walk on Boston Common in the issue for May 30 (1:1–2).

Nathaniel Whittier's recuperation is detailed in "A Remarkable Recovery," San Francisco *Alta California,* 20 September 1866, 1:1. As Harte had predicted in letter 17, the official inquiry into the collapse of the boarding house on Summer street concluded that there was no criminal liability (San Francisco *Bulletin,* 23 August 1866, 2:1).

The "disputable weekly" Harte mentions was *Puck,* which "appears to have been an advertising sheet for the questionable Pacific Museum of Anatomy" (Franklin Walker, *San Francisco's Literary Frontier* [New York: Knopf, 1939], p. 247). Harte alludes to the magazine again in letter 35. The paper "made popular by the sparkling pruriency of an eastern correspondent" was the *Sacramento Union* (*Springfield Republican,* 30 May 1866, 6:2). In its issue for 9 June 1866, the New York *Round Table* had described Charles Reade's sensational novel "Griffith Gaunt," under serialization in the *Atlantic Monthly,* as "grossly impure" and "indecent."

LETTER 20. The official results of the municipal election are reported in the San Francisco *Alta California,* 11 September 1866, 1:2–3.

Washington Irving's essay on "The Great Mississippi Bubble" originally appeared in the *Knickerbocker* for April 1840 and was collected in *Wolfert's Roost* in 1855.

The report of Professor Alphonse Wood, a Brooklyn botanist, before the California Academy of Sciences on September 3, including the paragraph Harte excerpts, appeared in the San Francisco *Bulletin* for 10 September 1866, 1:4.

LETTER 21. Dwinelle's oration is reprinted in its entirety in the San Francisco *Bulletin* for 10 September 1866, 5:3–7. A lengthy summary of Stebbins's sermon "Revivals" appears in the San Francisco *Daily American Flag* for 8 September 1866, 3:4. Henry W. Bellows (1814–1882), minister of All Souls Unitarian Church in New York, filled the pulpit at the First Unitarian Church in San Francisco between April and September 1864, the period between King's death and Stebbins's selection as his successor. He delivered the oration before the Society of Pioneers on 9 September 1864, shortly before his departure for the East (Walter Donald Kring, *Henry Whitney Bellows* [Boston: Skinner House, 1979], pp. 284–98).

LETTER 22. The description of a California resort in this letter, like the description of Mission Dolores in letter 6, echoes a sketch Harte had written earlier for the *Golden Era* (24 May 1863).

LETTER 23. Bishop Kip's letter to the *Pacific Churchman* is summarized at length in "The English Church at Honolulu," San Francisco *Call*, 30 September 1866, 1:1.

Queen Emma's reception is reported in the *Alta California*, 25 September 1866, 1:1; and her movements over the next two weeks are summarized in the *Bulletin*, 7 October 1866, 5:4.

LETTER 24. U. S. Grant had been stationed in San Francisco in 1852. W. T. Sherman had lived in San Francisco for two years in the 1840s, was stationed there in 1849, and had worked for a San Francisco bank for three years in the mid-1850s. E. D. Baker (1811–1861), a colonel and U. S. Senator from Oregon, died at Ball's Bluff in command of a "California regiment" recruited in New York and Pennsylvania. Henry W. Halleck (1815–1872) had helped draft the California state constitition in 1849 and commanded the Division of the Pacific at San Francisco in 1866. The travel writer Bayard Taylor (1825–1878) spent five months in California in 1849, an experience he subsequently chronicled in *Eldorado* (1850). Albert Bierstadt (1830–1902) first traveled to the West in 1858 and soon established his reputation as a landscape painter there. On Bierstadt, see also letter 33. Fitz Hugh Ludlow (1836–1870) traveled to California in 1863 for reasons of health, and his articles about the trip for the *Atlantic* were subsequently reprinted in *The Heart of the Continent* (1870). Schuyler Colfax of Indiana (1823–1885), Speaker of the House and Vice-President of the U. S. during the Crédit Mobilier scandal, led a party of prominent men across country to California in 1865. Horace Greeley (1811–1872), editor of the *New York Tribune*, traveled to the Pacific coast in 1859 and later published an account of his trip, *An Overland Journey from New York to San Francisco in the Summer of 1859* (1860). On Bellows, see the notes to letter

21 above. Samuel Bowles (1826–1878), editor and publisher of the *Springfield Republican*, traveled west in the Colfax party and wrote a series of letters about the trip for his newspaper, later collected under the title *Across the Continent* (1865). William Bross (1813–1890), the Lieutenant Governor of Illinois and one of the editors of the *Chicago Tribune*, also visited California in the Colfax party and also wrote a series of letters about the trip for his newspaper.

The judgement in the suit of the United States *vs.* Michael Reese, an off-spring of the Limantour episode, is reported in "Important Decision by Judge Field," San Francisco *Bulletin*, 24 September 1866, 5:5–6.

LETTER 25. The tremor on September 5 was detected by the *Imperial* at Kodiac island (San Francisco *Alta California*, 3 October 1866, 1:5) and by the whaling schooner *Caroline E. Foote* at sea (San Francisco *Bulletin*, 5 October 1866, 3:4). The accident aboard the *Julia* was detailed in the *Alta California*, 30 September 1866, 1:2; and in the *Bulletin*, 1 October 1866, 5:4. The clipper ship *Hornet* sank in open sea on 3 May 1866. Mark Twain reported the event in a piece entitled "Forty-Three Days in an Open Boat" in the *Sacramento Union* for 25 June 1866, reprinted with revisions in *Harper's* for December 1866; and he later reminisced about his scoop in *My Début as a Literary Person* (1903). Twain's may have been the "competent hands" Harte expected to edit Samuel Ferguson's journal.

Twain delivered his famous lecture on the Sandwich Islands—to tap interest sparked by the visit of Queen Emma—at Maguire's Opera House in San Francisco on 2 October 1866. See also chapter 78 in *Roughing It*. "Artemus Ward" was the pseudonym of Charles F. Browne (1834–1867), a humorist who toured the West in 1863–1864.

LETTER 26. Harte cites a reference to Queen Emma at Grace Cathedral which had appeared in the San Francisco *Daily American Flag* for 1 October 1866, 3:3. Kip's life is also sketched in the *Dictionary of American Biography*; and by Kevin Starr in *Americans and the California Dream 1850–1915*, pp. 83–85. Kip later contributed to the *Overland Monthly*, 2 (February 1869), 164–70; and 2 (May 1869), 401–12.

LETTER 27. A. B. Earle preached the first sermon in the revival on 7 October 1866 under the auspices of the San Francisco Ministerial Union (San Francisco *Bulletin*, 8 October 1866, 5:4). The meetings were held during the week and on Sunday afternoons in Platt's Hall and on Sunday evenings in Union Hall (*Bulletin*, 29 October 1866, 3:4).

LETTER 28. Some twenty-five or thirty Chinese day-laborers—under contract to a private contractor who paid each of them barely a dollar a day

—were working on Townsend street near Second when, in the morning of 12 February 1867, they were attacked by a mob of about four hundred whites. A Chinese bystander with "no connection with the work at South Beach" was nearly beaten to death (San Francisco *Alta California*, 13 February 1867, 1:1).

LETTER 29. The steamer *Colorado* docked in San Francisco on March 20 and departed for China again on April 3.

Before their departure on 30 March 1867, according to a report in the San Francisco *Bulletin*, the Japanese commissioners visited the U. S. Mint and were guests "at a private dinner party at R. B. Swain's" (29 March 1867, 3:6).

Caroline F. Clark had filed suit for breach of promise on 9 February 1866 (San Francisco *Bulletin*, 10 February 1866, 3:4). The trial occurred in late March 1867. The "case against another wealthy Californian" Harte mentions in the letter pitted the widow Schell against General Naglee (San Francisco *Dramatic Chronicle*, 4 May 1867, 2:1). Ironically, the transcript of the Reese *vs.* Clark divorce trial was parodied as "condensed a la 'Bret'" in "Ye Melancholie Romaunt of Michael Reese," *Dramatic Chronicle*, 22 March 1867, 2:1.

A series of meetings were held in the city in early April to raise money on behalf of destitute black and white Southerners. See also the notes to letter 30.

LETTER 30. A meeting to raise funds for Southern relief was held at the Academy of Music on 4 April 1867. The speeches by Reverends Cohn, O. P. Fitzgerald, and Stone were summarized in the San Francisco *Bulletin* for 5 April 1867, 3:3. R. B. Swain and Leland Stanford were selected vice-presidents of the committee at the same meeting.

The Chandler-Harris fight was originally scheduled for 11 April 1867 at an amphitheatre in San Mateo county between the San Bruno turnpike and Seventeen Mile House. At 9:40 A.M., a train of thirteen passenger cars crowded with about a thousand passengers left the San Jose station on Market street in San Francisco for the site. At about 2:20 P.M., Sheriff Lathrop of San Mateo country entered the ring to prevent the fight (San Francisco *Bulletin*, 11 April 1867, 3:5). The "picnic" then took place on Saturday, April 13, near Sausalito, and lasted twenty-three rounds, with Chandler the victor (*Bulletin*, 15 April 1867, 3:3–4).

A Democrat and professional gambler, John Morrissey was a Congressman from California, the subject of a satirical essay signed "B. H." in the San Francisco *Alta California* for 11 November 1866, 2:2. This essay has not been previously listed in bibliographies of Harte's works.

Mark Twain also refers in chapter 56 of *Roughing It* to the "snow-walled curves of the Pacific Railroad" in the mountains of central California.

LETTER 31. The annual celebration of Cinco de Mayo was reported on 7 May 1867 in both the *Alta California* (1:2) and the *Bulletin* (3:6).

A former Douglas Democrat, John Conness was elected in 1862 as a Union Democrat to a single six-year term in the U. S. Senate. John Bidwell had lived in California since 1841 and he had been one of the first settlers to publicize the discovery of gold in 1848. Frank M. Pixley had been elected state attorney general as a Republican in 1861. Caleb T. Fay ran for mayor of San Francisco on the Republican ticket in 1860 and was elected to the office as a Unionist in 1862. Bidwell, Pixley, and Fay were each running for governor in 1867. They are also mentioned in letters 32 and 34.

The *Oriflamme* is described in detail in the San Francisco *Daily American Flag* for 21 June 1866, 1:1.

LETTER 32. The machinations of the gubernatorial campaign of 1867 —which Harte also discusses in letter 34—are summarized in *The Rumble of California Politics 1848–1970*, ed. Royce D. Delmatier *et al.* (New York: Wiley, 1970), pp. 56–59. Harte's account of George C. Gorham's career is not entirely accurate: Gorham had been appointed superintendent of the state reform school in 1862, clerk of the U. S. circuit court in 1863, and private secretary to Governor F. F. Low in 1864.

LETTER 33. Bierstadt's "Domes of the Yosemite," his largest canvas to date, was commissioned by Legrand Lockwood and completed in 1867. It is now located in the St. Johnsbury Atheneum in St. Johnsbury, Vermont (George Hendricks, *A. Bierstadt* [Fort Worth: Amon Carter Museum, 1972], pp. 22–25).

LETTER 34. Henry H. Haight (1825–1878) graduated from Yale in 1844 and emigrated to California in 1850. Originally a Free-Soiler, then a Democrat, the chair of the state Republican party by 1859, he was elected governor on the Democratic ticket in 1867 by advocating restricted Chinese immigration and the eight-hour working day and opposing black suffrage. In retrospect, Harte's conclusion that the "decease of the Union party of California will be traced primarily to corruption" seems fair and accurate. As H. H. Bancroft noted, the party "had been guided and directed by pure men and patriots" during the Civil War, but after the armistice "tricksters . . . forced many of the best men out" of the party (*The Works of Hubert Howe Bancroft* [San Francisco: History Company, 1890], XXIV, 326).

LETTER 35. Harte's column is apparently inspired by "Manufacture of Books in California," an editorial in the San Francisco *Bulletin* for 17 August 1867, 2:2. "John Phœnix" was the *nom de plume* of George H. Derby (1823–1861), who has been credited with developing a boisterous Western style of humor writing. *Vanity Fair* was edited by "Artemus Ward" (Charles F. Browne).

The Rev. A. W. Loomis's *Confucius and the Chinese Classics* is reviewed in the San Francisco *Bulletin* for 17 August 1867, 1:1–2. According to Franklin Walker, Harte was responsible for the selection of Stoddard's *Poems* (*San Francisco's Literary Frontier*, p. 230). Stoddard later became a regular contributor to the *Overland Monthly*. Harte also refers to reviews of Stoddard's *Poems* which had appeared in the *Bulletin* for 24 August 1867, 1:1–2; and the *Californian*—this one written by the editor James P. Bowman—for 31 August 1867, p. 8.

LETTER 36. Harte cites an essay on "The Upper Yellowstone" which had appeared in the *Montana Post* for 31 August 1867, 6:1.

The Ha-yah-ta-kee acrobatic troupe, which the *Alta California* claimed "to surpass all others" (16 September 1867, 1:3), opened at the Metropolitan Theatre in San Francisco on 23 September 1867. The next evening, during its second performance in the city, according to local papers dated September 25, the acrobats introduced into their routine "an unpardonable vulgarity" (*Alta California*, 1:3), an "indescribable vulgarity" (*Dramatic Chronicle*, 3:1), "an indecency perhaps unparalleled on any stage" (*Bulletin*, 3:3). Harte's allusion to the brothel at Pompeii echoes, if in a different context, a paragraph in Mark Twain's letter on the buried city in the *Alta California*, 29 September 1867, 1:4.

The so-called "Pueblo movement" had been in the news for over a month before Harte mentions it. See "Pueblo Land Organization," *Bulletin*, 26 August 1867, 3:3–5; and "Pueblo Land Question," *Alta California*, 3 October 1867, 1:2.

According to the *Alta California*, the *Nightingale* docked in San Francisco on October 8 with "the bulk of the Russian Overland Telegraph party" (9 October 1867, 1:8). The same paper reported the donation of the College of California property to the State Agricultural, Mining and Mechanical College on October 9 (10 October 1867, 1:2). The *Bulletin* soon endorsed the proposal to establish a state university on the donated land (2 November 1867, 2:2).

LETTER 37. According to the *Bulletin* for 9 November 1867, 3:5, Stebbins was conducting Sunday evening services in the Metropolitan Theatre in the city.

INDEX

A. Roman & Co., 140
abolitionism, 83, 128
Academy of Music, 162
Across the Continent (Bowles), 7, 161
Adams, John, 32
Addison, Joseph, 92
Agassiz, Louis, 63
agriculture, 27, 44, 58–59, 62, 90–91, 133–34
Alaska, 102, 119, 127, 147
Alcatraces island, 99, 131
Alexander VI, Pope, 87
American Literature, 10
American River, 112
American Unitarian Association, 157
Ames, Charles G., 20, 24, 50, 61, 96, 153
Associated Alumni of the Pacific Coast, 45, 155
Atlantic Monthly, 2, 159
Auzerais House (San Jose), 135

Baker, E. D., 98, 160
Bancroft, H. H., 163
Barbary Coast, 125
Bell, G. W., 36, 38
Bellows, Henry, 86, 88, 89, 98, 153, 160
Berkeley, Cal., 4, 72–73, 158
Bidwell, John, 126, 129, 136, 163
Bierstadt, Albert, 98, 133, 160, 163
Bloomerism, 3, 74–75, 158–59

Bolander, Prof., 57–58
Boston Common, 78, 159
Boston Transcript, 2
Bowles, Samuel, 6–9, 98, 161
Bowman, James P., 164
Branch, Edgar M., 157
breach of promise suits, 118–19, 162
Breckinridge, John C., 82
Brewster, John, Jr., 67, 68
Brooks, C. W., 31
Bross, William, 6, 98, 161
Brotherton, Thomas W., 156
Brown, John, 83
Browne, Charles F. *See* Ward, Artemus.
Buchanan, James, 117
bull-fight, 22
Burlingame, Anson, 28, 31, 154
Byron, Lord, 84

California Academy of Natural Sciences, 57, 157, 159
California gubernatorial campaign of 1867, 127–29, 135–37, 163
California state assembly, 30–31, 154
California state fair, 90–91
California State Geological Survey, 57
Californian, 1, 5, 6, 144
Camanche, 53, 157
Cambon, Benito, 32
"Cardinal Richelieu" (Bulwer-Lytton), 46, 155–56

Caroline E. Foote, 102, 161
Cartro, Manuel, 99
Central Park (New York), 3, 72
Chandler, Tommy, 121, 162
Chicago Tribune, 161
children, 79, 93
Chinese New Year, 27, 154
"Chinese question," 31, 113–15, 138
"Christabel" (Coleridge), 133
Christian Commission, 48, 119
Church of England, 75–77, 95, 98, 105
Cinco de Mayo, 123, 162
City Gardens (San Francisco), 149
Clark, Caroline F., 118–19, 162
Clemens, Samuel L. *See* Twain, Mark.
Cliff House, 61
climate, 21, 26–27, 31–32, 41, 43–44, 51, 61, 72, 73–74, 78–79, 101, 112, 122, 126–27, 130–31
Coast Range, 57, 132, 133, 134
Cohn, Rabbi, 120, 162
Coleridge, Samuel T., 125, 133
Colfax, Schuyler, 6, 98, 160, 161
College of California, 8, 45, 72, 147–48, 155, 164
Colorado, 115–16, 162
Confucius and the Chinese Classics (ed. Loomis), 140–42, 163
Congress Springs, Cal., 103
Conness, John, 125–26, 128, 137, 163
Contra Costa, Cal., 21
Cowing, Turner, 158
Crédit Mobilier, 160

Dane, G. Ezra, 159
Davis, Jefferson, 50, 82
Day, A. Grove, 159
Dayton, Oh., 56
De Quincy, Thomas, 40, 53

Deaf and Dumb Asylum (San Francisco), 49
Delmatier, Royce D., 163
Derby, George H. See Phœnix, John.
DeWolf, Eliza, 158–59
Dictionary of American Biography, 153, 161
diseases, 43–44, 73–74, 92, 131
"Domes of the Yosemite" (Bierstadt), 133, 163
Draper, John W., 27, 31, 154
Duane, Charles, 53–54, 157
Duane, John, 157
Dwinelle, John, 86–88, 129, 158, 160

Earle, A. B., 5, 108–11, 145, 161
earthquakes, 28–30, 41–42, 43, 52, 63, 68, 74, 79, 102, 145, 154, 161
Ellis, Moses, 19
"Endymion" (Lyly), 101

Fay, Caleb T., 126, 136, 137, 163
Ferguson, Samuel, 103, 161
Field, Judge, 128, 161
Fields, Annie, 158
Fields, James T., 2, 158
Fields, Osgood & Co., 1
First Congregational Church (San Francisco), 24, 60, 150, 154
First Unitarian Church (San Francisco), 1–2, 7, 13, 19–20, 56, 150, 153
Fitzgerald, O. P., 120, 162
floods, 112
Forrest, Edwin, 1, 15, 46, 54, 155–56, 157
Fourth of July 1866 celebration, 51–52, 55–56, 82–83, 156–57
Fussell, Edwin, 9

Geysers, 131, 157
Golden Era, 1, 155

Gorham, George C., 126, 128–29, 136, 137, 138, 163
Grace Cathedral (San Francisco), 105, 150, 161
Grant, U. S., 98, 160
"Great Mississippi Bubble, The" (Irving), 83, 159
Greeley, Horace, 6, 98, 160
Griffith Gaunt (Reade), 81, 159
Gulliver's Travels (Swift), 41

Haight, Henry, 137, 163
Halleck, Henry W., 98, 160
Hamlet (Shakespeare), 32, 80
Hancock, John, 32
Harris, Doony, 121, 162
Harte, Anna Griswold (wife), 5
Harte, F. Bret. Payment received for California correspondence, 1, 6. Works: "At the Sepulchre" (poem), 2; "Bohemian Days in San Francisco" (essay), 158; "Colonel Starbottle for the Plaintiff," 5; "Legend of Monte del Diablo, The," 2; *Luck of Roaring Camp and Other Sketches, The,* 4–5; "Luck of Roaring Camp, The," 8; "Maruja," 5; "Miggles," 8; "Mission Dolores" (essay), 4; "Mr. MacGlowrie's Widow," 5; "Mr. Thompson's Prodigal," 8; "On a Pen of Thomas Starr King" (poem), 2; "Outcasts of Poker Flat, The," 5, 8; *Outcroppings* (edited anthology), 5, 8, 154, 155; "Plain Language from Truthful James" (poem), 4, 8; "Reformation of James Reddy, The," 5; "Relieving Guard" (poem), 2; "Tennessee's Partner," 8; "To the Pliocene Skull" (poem), 5; "Wan Lee, the Pagan," 4, 154

Harte, Francis King (son), 2
Harvard College, 45
Hawthorne, Nathaniel, 65, 158
Hayes' Park (San Francisco), 149
Hecht, T. E., 14–17
Hendricks, George, 163
Higby, William, 126
highwaymen, 39–40
Hill, J. B., 50, 156
Hittell, J. S., 140
Hornet, 103, 161
Howard Presbyterian Church (San Francisco), 155
Howe, M. A. DeW., 158
Howells, W. D., 9
Hugo, Victor, 116
Humboldt Co., Cal., 3
humor, 31

"Il Travatore," 74
Imperial, 102, 161
infant mortality, 79
Irish in California, 4, 51–52, 114, 128
Irving, Washington, 83, 159

Japanese acrobats, 1, 145–47, 164
Japanese diplomats, 97–98, 116–18, 162
Jefferson, Thomas, 83
Jewish Synagogue (San Francisco), 150
Johnson, Andrew, 24–25, 82, 126, 136, 154
Julia, 102–3, 161

King, Thomas Starr, 1–2, 5, 6, 13, 20, 23–24, 56, 73, 82, 88, 89, 94–96, 106, 119, 120, 137, 150, 151, 153, 160
Kip, William Ingraham, 49–50, 105, 106–7, 108, 120, 150, 156, 160, 161

Kodiac island, 102, 161
Knickerbocker, 159
Knight, Samuel, 37–38
Kring, Walter, 160
"Kubla Khan" (Coleridge), 141

Lacey, E. J., 24, 59–60, 154
Latham, Milton G., 137
Lathrop, Sheriff, 121, 162
Limantour, Jose Y., 99–100, 161
Lincoln, Abraham, 31, 137
Lockwood, Legrand, 163
Lone Mountain, 34, 124
Long Bridge, 125
Longfellow, Henry Wadsworth, 155
Loomis, A. W., 141, 163
Los Angeles, Cal., 131
Low, F. F., 128, 163
Lowell, James Russell, 104
Ludlow, Fitz Hugh, 98, 160

Macbeth (Shakespeare), 81, 154
McCarthy, Daniel O., 129, 130, 154
McClellan, George B., 82
McCready, Willie, 67, 68
Maguire's Opera House, 15, 46,
    155–56, 161
Mare island, 53
Matson, James, 62
Maximilian, 123
Mechanics' Institute, 64
Mercantile Library, 64, 153
Merchants' Exchange, 63, 64
Metropolitan Theatre (San Fran-
    cisco), 164
Mission Dolores, 4, 32–35, 87, 149,
    155, 160
Mission Peak, 21
Monadnock, 53, 157
Montana Post, 1, 144, 164
Monte del Diablo, 21
Monterey, Cal., 44, 87
Monthly Journal, 61, 157

Moore, Thomas, 84
Mormons, 27
Morrissey, John, 122, 162
Mount Hood, 85–86, 89
Mount Shasta, 21, 89, 131
Munchausen, Baron, 122
murders, 52–53
My Début as a Literary Person (Twain),
    161

Naglee, General, 162
Nation, 31–32, 154–55
New York *Evening Post,* 129
New York Herald, 129
New York Times, 5, 31–32, 155
New York Tribune, 160
Nightingale, 147, 164
nitro-glycerine, 36–38, 52, 66, 67,
    102, 145

Oakland, Cal., 45, 72, 86
Oakland News, 86
Occidental Hotel, 17, 97
Olmstead, Frederick Law, 3, 64, 72,
    158
Oriflamme, 127, 163
Overland Monthly, 8, 9, 153, 158, 161,
    164

Pacific, 49, 60
Pacific Board of Brokers, 83–84,
    100
Pacific Churchman, 49, 50, 94–95,
    156, 160
Pacific Museum of Anatomy, 159
Palou, Francisco, 32, 87
Passages from the English Note-Books
    (Hawthorne), 158
Peto, Sir Morton, 59
Phœnix, John, 139, 163
Pixley, Frank, 126, 129, 163
Placerville, Cal., 136
Platt's Hall (San Francisco), 161

pliocene skull, 5, 62–63, 86, 158
Poems of Charles Warren Stoddard, The,
    140, 142–44, 164
Pomona, Cal., 78
Pompeii, 146, 164
Port Oxford, Cal., 44
Portland, Me., 54, 56, 153, 157
Potter, Bishop, 107
Presidio, 87
prize fight, 121–122
"Psalm of Life, The" (Longfellow),
    155
Puck, 80, 139, 140, 159
Pueblo land dispute, 87, 147, 164

Queen Emma, 1, 17, 96, 97–98,
    103–4, 160, 161

race discrimination, 3–4, 28, 51–
    52, 55–56, 113–14, 128, 156–57,
    161–62
Reade, Charles, 159
redwoods, 57–58, 132
Reese, Michael, 99, 118–19, 161, 162
Reese River Reveille, 65
resorts, 22, 44, 91–94, 160
revivals, 88, 108–11
Richardson, A. D., 6
"Rip Van Winkle" (Irving), 83
Rodgers, John, 53, 157
Ross, William G., 53, 157
Roughing It (Twain), 6, 155, 161, 162
Round Table, 81, 159

Sacramento, Cal., 24, 50, 61, 90, 96,
    156
Sacramento River, 112
Sacramento Union, 1, 5, 104, 126, 129,
    136, 159, 161
St. James's Church (San Francisco),
    50, 105, 156
St. Johnsbury Athenaeum, 163

San Francisco *Alta California,* 1, 7,
    129, 136, 155, 162, 164
San Francisco Board of Supervisors,
    37, 64–65, 69
San Francisco *Daily American Flag,*
    129, 154, 160, 161
San Francisco *Evening Bulletin,* 1, 7,
    129, 136, 144, 154, 157, 158, 159,
    160, 162, 164
San Francisco in 1866 (ed. Stewart
    and Fussell), 9–10
San Francisco Ministerial Union, 52,
    55, 161
San Francisco *Morning Call,* 1, 7,
    69–70, 129, 136
San Francisco municipal election of
    1866, 82, 138, 159
San Jose, Cal., 134–35
San Mateo Co., Cal., 121, 162
Sandwich Islands, 75–77, 94–96,
    104, 139, 159, 161
Santa Clara valley, 134
Santa Cruz, Cal., 44, 50, 96
Sartor Resartus (Carlyle), 124
Sausalito, Cal., 126, 162
Sawyer, Warren, 6
Scudder, Henry M., 45, 111, 155
Serra, Junípero, 33
Seventeen Mile House, 162
Seward, William, 25, 45, 96, 98
Shafter, Oscar L., 45, 155
Sherman, William T., 98, 160
Shubrick, 104
slaughter houses, 125
Society of California Pioneers, 63,
    86–88, 160
South Beach (San Francisco), 125,
    162
Southern Relief Committee, 119–20,
    127, 162
Staley, Bishop, 75–77, 94–95, 98,
    105
Stanford, Leland, 162

Starr, Kevin, 153, 161
State Agricultural, Mining and Mechanical College, 164
steamer day, 38
Stebbins, Horatio, 6, 19–20, 24–26, 31, 45, 49, 50, 56, 73, 86, 88–89, 106, 109, 120, 151–52, 153, 160, 164
Stewart, George R., Jr., 9–10, 158
stock gambling, 57, 83–85, 100
Stockton, Cal., 61, 102
Stoddard, Charles W., 140, 142–44, 164
Stone, A. L., 24, 28, 47–49, 52, 55, 106, 111, 120, 150, 151, 154, 156–57, 162
suicide, 57, 85, 148, 157
Summer Street House, 66–72, 79–80, 102, 159
Sunday question, 47–49, 151, 156
Swain, Robert B., 5, 20, 120, 153, 162
Swinburne, A. C., 41

Tamalpais, Cal., 126
Taylor, Bayard, 98, 160
Telegraph Hill, 14, 74, 123, 124
temperance, 40
Tempest, The (Shakespeare), 154
Thomson, James, 41
Trinity Church (San Francisco), 150
Trinity island, 102
Tupper, Martin, 117
Twain, Mark, 1, 6, 7, 15, 75–77, 104, 139, 155, 159, 161, 162, 164

Union College, 45
Union Hall (San Francisco), 161
Union Pacific railroad, 30
Union Party of California, 82, 127–28, 129, 138

United States Mint (San Francisco Branch), 5, 7, 162
United States Sanitary Commission, 2, 56, 57, 120, 127

Van Valkenburgh, R. B., 28, 31, 154
Vanderbilt, 53, 96, 103, 157
Vanity Fair, 139, 163
Venard, Stephen, 5, 39–40
Vermehr, Rev., 108
vigilance committee, 53, 54, 128, 138, 157
Virginia City, Nev., 54, 56
voter registration, 46, 155

Wadsworth, Charles, 150
Walker, Franklin, 159, 164
Walton, Isaac, 86
Ward, Artemus, 104, 161, 163
Webb, C. H., 5–6, 7–8, 155
Wells, Fargo & Co., 35–38, 39, 66, 67, 155
Wendte, Charles W., 13, 153
Western Union, 147
Whitney, J. D., 62, 157
Whittier, Nathaniel, 68, 79, 159
Williams, Andrew, 45, 155
wines, 59–61
Wolfert's Roost (Irving), 159
Wood, Alphonse, 85–86, 159
Woodworth's Gardens, 149
Wyllie, W. C., 95

Xanadu, 72, 83

Yale College, 45
Yellowstone, 144–45, 164
Yo Semite, 27, 132, 133

Zion Methodist Church (San Francisco), 56, 157